THE EIGHTEENTH–CENTURY REVOLUTION

French or Western?

PROBLEMS IN EUROPEAN CIVILIZATION

UNDER THE EDITORIAL DIRECTION OF

Ralph W. Greenlaw and Dwight E. Lee†*

DECLINE AND FALL OF THE ROMAN EMPIRE—WHY DID IT COLLAPSE?†

THE PIRENNE THESIS—ANALYSIS, CRITICISM, AND REVISION*

THE CORONATION OF CHARLEMAGNE—WHAT DID IT SIGNIFY?*

THE RENAISSANCE—MEDIEVAL OR MODERN?*

MACHIAVELLI—CYNIC, PATRIOT, OR POLITICAL SCIENTIST?*

THE REFORMATION—MATERIAL OR SPIRITUAL?*

PROTESTANTISM AND CAPITALISM—THE WEBER THESIS AND ITS CRITICS*

THE ORIGINS OF THE ENGLISH CIVIL WAR—CONSPIRACY, CRUSADE, OR CLASS CONFLICT?*

THE REVOLUTION OF 1688—WHIG TRIUMPH OR PALACE REVOLUTION?†

THE GREATNESS OF LOUIS XIV—MYTH OR REALITY?*

THE EIGHTEENTH-CENTURY REVOLUTION—FRENCH OR WESTERN?†

THE ECONOMIC ORIGINS OF THE FRENCH REVOLUTION—POVERTY OR PROSPERITY?*

METTERNICH, THE "COACHMAN OF EUROPE"—STATESMAN OR EVIL GENIUS?*

THE INDUSTRIAL REVOLUTION IN BRITAIN—TRIUMPH OR DISASTER?*

1848—A TURNING POINT?*

OTTO VON BISMARCK—A HISTORICAL ASSESSMENT*

THE "NEW IMPERIALISM"—ANALYSIS OF LATE NINETEENTH-CENTURY EXPANSION*

THE OUTBREAK OF THE FIRST WORLD WAR—WHO WAS RESPONSIBLE?*

THE RUSSIAN REVOLUTION AND BOLSHEVIK VICTORY—WHY AND HOW?*

THE VERSAILLES SETTLEMENT—WAS IT FOREDOOMED TO FAILURE?*

THE ETHIOPIAN CRISIS—TOUCHSTONE OF APPEASEMENT?*

THE NAZI REVOLUTION—GERMANY'S GUILT OR GERMANY'S FATE?*

THE BRITISH IN INDIA—IMPERIALISM OR TRUSTEESHIP?†

THE OUTBREAK OF THE SECOND WORLD WAR—DESIGN OR BLUNDER?†

Other volumes in preparation

PROBLEMS IN EUROPEAN CIVILIZATION

THE EIGHTEENTH-CENTURY REVOLUTION

French or Western?

EDITED WITH AN INTRODUCTION BY

Peter Amann

MICHIGAN STATE UNIVERSITY OAKLAND

D. C. HEATH AND COMPANY · BOSTON

Library of Congress Catalog Card Number 63-9700

PRINTED IN THE UNITED STATES OF AMERICA

Table of Contents

Introduction

THE late eighteenth century used to be called the "Age of the French Revolution." Many historians continue to believe that the great dramatic events in France of the 1790's dominate the history of this period. During the last twenty years, however, a broader interpretation of the late eighteenth century has gained ground among certain American and French historians, of whom R. R. Palmer is the most articulate. Drawing on the insights gained from the twentieth-century world, in which international revolutions and supra-national blocs have become a commonplace, they have sought to reappraise the currents of the eighteenth century from the point of view of a common Western or Atlantic civilization. They are testing a working hypothesis drawn from contemporary experience by applying it to the revolutionary experience of two hundred years ago. Their reassessment of the eighteenth century in terms of a "Democratic Revolution of the West"—the thesis which this volume explores—was evidently suggested by the turmoil of yet another revolutionary age, our own.

This shift in emphasis from an "Age of the French Revolution" to an "Age of the Democratic Revolution of the West" raises at least three major problems of historical interpretation. First, was there indeed a truly supra-national revolutionary movement best studied from a Western rather than a national vantage point? Secondly, international or not, are these revolutions best described as "democratic"? Thirdly, even admitting the significance of several revolutions, is revolution the dominant and most meaningful feature of the late eighteenth century?

The factual evidence cited in support of the thesis of an international eighteenth-century revolution is not in dispute. It is undeniable that from the 1760's to the turn of the century, Europe and its transatlantic annex witnessed an astonishing number of political conflicts which may be called revolutionary. The tiny city-state of Geneva was in intermittent turmoil in the 1760's, the 1780's, and again after 1792. The Revolutionary War of the Thirteen Colonies which broke out in the mid-seventies hardly needs a commentary. In 1780, Ireland, and even England, appeared on the verge of major disturbances, if not of revolution. A few years later the Netherlands underwent revolutionary conflict which was ultimately crushed by Prussian intervention. The aristocratic phase of the French Revolution began, according to most historians, in 1787. Two years later, not only did the French Revolution broaden into a mass movement, but there were revolutionary outbreaks at the two extremities of the Hapsburg Monarchy: Hungary and the Austrian Netherlands. From the time of the First Partition in 1772, Poland experienced intermittent reform movements of revolutionary proportions that reached their tragic climax between 1791 and 1794. Holland entered yet another revolutionary phase in 1795. From 1797 on, Italy, Switzerland, and parts of western Germany all had revolutions, supported, but not necessarily instigated, by the victorious armies of the French Republic.

If the facts themselves are scarcely in dispute, the same cannot be said of their interpretation. Aside from the three major problems raised earlier, a host of other questions present themselves to the student of the Palmer thesis. Is such a proliferation of revolutions really so unique? Could one not find, as R. B. Merriman has sought to do for the mid-seventeenth century, many other "ages of revolution"? Save for brief intervals, has there ever been a period of modern Western history that has not been an "age of revolution"? Is it possible, moreover, to talk in the same breath of municipal strife in Geneva and of the French Revolution? Of militia unrest in Ireland and of the American Revolution? Are these simultaneous movements really of a comparable order of magnitude? Are they best understood as parts of a vast occidental upheaval, or as specific products of a specific historical environment?

The historians or pamphleteers who sought to interpret their own age for their eighteenth-century contemporaries disagreed sharply over the import and consequences of what they had witnessed. Yet regardless of ideological convictions, most of them viewed the revolutionary conflicts from a cosmopolitan, non-national point of view, though they had to explain the pre-eminence of the revolution in France. If these eighteenth-century analysts were pioneering proponents of an international viewpoint, their consensus is inconclusive: the eighteenth-century supra-national approach may merely testify to the cosmopolitanism of the intellectuals of the day.

As the generation which had lived through the revolutions died off, national historians replaced international-minded propagandists. Frenchmen and Americans, regardless of ideological predilections, were interested in their own French or American revolutions, not in some vague international movement of which these might have been a part. Revolutionary historiography tended to become rigidly national in perspective. Particularly in France, this nationalism was reinforced by the demands of domestic politics, since histories of the Great Revolution served as weapons in the ideological and party struggles of the Third Republic. Under these circumstances, it was not surprising that neither historians nor readers showed much interest in viewing their cherished or abhorred national pasts in the broader spectrum of occidental civilization.

The revival of a supra-national interpretation of the revolutions of the eighteenth century was perhaps not unrelated to the crisis of the national state in the twentieth century. Fascist and Communist ideologies were to pose the problem of the international character of revolutionary movements. No doubt the defensive unity of the West since the Second World War, symbolized by NATO, has also contributed to a reappraisal of the West's eighteenth-century revolutionary experience in terms of its essential unity.

The selections in this volume, drawn from twentieth-century analyses of the eighteenth century, are organized into three parts. The first of these offers Palmer's interpretation of the latter part of the eighteenth century as an "age of the democratic revolution," followed by critical appraisals of this thesis. The selections of Part II analyze a number of individual eighteenth-century revolutions which Palmer had cited as evidence. Two of the articles examine the relationship between the two major revolutions of the eighteenth century, the American and the French. Finally, the essays in Part III suggest alternative perspectives on the eighteenth century and its revolutions.

In his article "The World Revolution of the West: 1763–1801," Palmer suggests some major unifying themes justifying a supra-national interpretation of the eighteenth-century revolutions. In the realm of ideas, he points to the demand for personal autonomy; in the area of class, to a parallel revolutionary surge of nobility and bourgeoisie; in the area of international relations, to a ubiquitous interaction of revolution and war. The selection from

The Age of the Democratic Revolution presents Palmer's characterization of the eighteenth-century revolution as specifically "democratic."

Cobban, while agreeing with the major conclusions of *The Age of the Democratic Revolution,* remains unpersuaded by the evidence marshalled in support of the thesis of a universal Western revolution. There are, in Cobban's view, too many far-fetched parallels in Palmer's comparative history of the eighteenth century, as well as too much slurring over of contrasts. One area of the attempted synthesis, Cobban maintains—the crucial evolution of popular sovereignty from theory to practice—remains altogether fragmentary.

Reinhard's criticism goes beyond methods to the very crux of Palmer's thesis. The stress on the occidental character of the eighteenth-century revolutions distorts our perspective, Reinhard asserts, by exaggerating common denominators at the expense of the more significant specific differences in the scope and nature of revolutionary phenomena. The French Revolution, for example, displays an egalitarian drive which completely overshadows that of any other contemporary upheaval.

Cobb's "The English Jacobins and the French Revolution" squarely challenges the authenticity of the English exhibit in Palmer's gallery of the "World Revolution of the West." What Cobb seeks to prove is that there was no "revolutionary situation" in England, that indeed the English Jacobins were no more than voices crying in the wilderness.

Calkin, on the other hand, stresses the inspiration to genuine Irish revolutionaries of the principles and example of the French Revolution, despite the handicap of the French revolutionary anti-clericalism and the ultimate failure of the Irish revolutionary movement of the 1790's.

By contrast, Wangermann, in his study of Jacobinism in the Hapsburg Monarchy during the same period, minimizes the scope and organization of revolutionary activities. The so-called "Jacobin Conspiracy," he holds, was little more than an attempt to organize and coordinate political opposition to the reactionary policies of the Hapsburg Monarchy after Leopold II's death.

Palmer, in his examination of the Dutch Revolution, not unnaturally confirms his own thesis. Despite local peculiarities and a characteristic moderation, the Dutch Revolution displayed some of the same egalitarian aspirations of other eighteenth-century revolutions, expressed in analogous constitutional terms, and evoked a typical counterrevolutionary reaction.

Tolles's reconsideration of the American Revolution as a social movement raises the somewhat different, but equally relevant, issue as to the "democratic" nature of one of Palmer's show pieces in the "World Revolution of the West." In an appraisal of the American Revolution as a democratic movement, Tolles concludes that the revolution had far less social content than historians such as Jameson had assumed.

From a very different standpoint, Gottschalk seeks to define the relationship of the American to the French Revolution. Unlike Palmer on the lookout for common denominators, Gottschalk seeks merely to define the role of the American Revolution in bringing on the French Revolution.

Boutmy, whose concern is ideological, dissociates the French from the American Revolution altogether. By a close textual comparison of the basic documents of both revolutions—the Declaration of Independence and the Declaration of the Rights of Man—Boutmy claims to demonstrate the narrowly legalistic approach of the American revolutionists in contrast to the universalism of the French revolutionaries.

What Tolles did for the American Revolution, Cobban does for the French by raising the question: how revolutionary was the French Revolution? From a detailed analysis of the personnel of the revolutionary legislative assemblies, Cobban concludes that the "democratic" impact of the revolution was confined, aside from freeing the peasants from annoying manorial dues, to opening a fuller career for a host of minor officials.

Like Palmer, Lefebvre interprets the latter eighteenth century as a revolutionary era; yet unlike Palmer he draws a clear-cut distinction between the Anglo-Saxon revolutions in which nobility and bourgeoisie combined against royal absolutism and the French Revolution in which the bourgeoisie, facing a united front of monarch and aristocracy, was forced into more egalitarian channels.

For Göhring, on the contrary, if the late eighteenth century was an age of dynamic change, of rapid modernization, it was not one of revolution. The characteristic means of effecting social reform were through enlightened absolutism. Only in France had royal absolutism grown so feeble and irresolute as to be unable to enforce needed reforms. The French Revolution thus appears not as the core of an occidental revolution, but as an anomaly, a breach in the solid front of reform from above.

Palmer, summing up his thesis in the face of criticism, not only stresses the peculiar significance of the American Revolution as an indispensable link in the revolutionary chain, but also admits the uniqueness of the French Revolution as the only eighteenth-century revolution accomplished without outside aid.

While agreeing in the main with Palmer, Godechot underlines the universality of the revolution (the time limits of which he extended from 1801 to 1849), rather than its "democratic" character. While admitting the preponderant role of the United States and France, Godechot, like Palmer, conceives of a supra-national movement with a scope much broader than these two countries.

These essays offer a number of modern interpretations of the late eighteenth century, accompanied by some of the evidence which they claim as their bases. In retrospect, it may be worth restating the essential questions which each critical reader must raise and answer for himself: (1) Was there an occidental revolution in the eighteenth century? (2) Was this revolution "democratic"? (3) Was revolution the dominant theme of the age?

CHRONOLOGY OF EIGHTEENTH-CENTURY REVOLUTIONS

1764–65 North America: British Sugar, Colonial Currency, Stamp, Quartering Acts. Declaration of Rights and Liberties by Stamp Act Congress (1765).

1768 Geneva: "Bourgeois" revolution broadening political base among citizens.

1774 North America: Meeting of First Continental Congress.

1775–83 North America: American Colonies' War for Independence.

1776–77 North America: Declaration of Independence and Articles of Confederation.

1780–85 England, Ireland: Climax of movement for parliamentary reform.

1782 Geneva: Counterrevolution reversing achievements of 1768.

1785–87 Netherlands: Dutch Patriot (anti-Orange) Party crushed by Prussian intervention in 1787.

1787 North America: Meeting of Constitutional Convention in Philadelphia.

France: Assembly of Notables called and dismissed by French king.

1789 Belgium: Uprising of the Austrian Netherlands against Joseph II's annulment of its privileges.

France: Calling of Estates General; elaboration of the first French Constitution (1789–91).

England: Agitation by English revolutionary clubs (1789–94).

1790 Belgium: Defeat of democratic revolutionary faction, followed by restoration of Hapsburg rule.

Hungary: Peasant insurrection against nobles; abortive aristocratic revolution against Hapsburgs.

1791 Geneva: Revolution leading to Constitution of 1791.

Poland: Polish Constitution of 1791.

1792 France: Abolition of monarchy; succeeded by republic.

1793 France: Revolutionary government—"advanced" Constitution of 1793 never put into effect.

1794 GENEVA: Inauguration of revolutionary government on the French model.

POLAND: National uprising under Kosciuszko defeated, followed by third and final partition of Poland (1795).

1795 NETHERLANDS: Inauguration of the Batavian Republic, lasting till 1806.

FRANCE: Inauguration of moderate republic: the Directory.

1797 ENGLAND: Large-scale mutinies in the British fleet with revolutionary overtones.

ITALY: French found Cisalpine, Ligurian republics.

1798 SWITZERLAND: Helvetic Republic instituted under French protection.

IRELAND: Unsuccessful revolutionary attempt with French aid.

ITALY: French found Roman Republic.

The Conflict of Opinion

I. The Palmer Thesis: Presentation and Criticism

"It may be that we should try to develop some integrating or unifying conceptions for this whole revolutionary movement in Europe and America taken together. . . . It is held that this . . . movement was essentially "democratic" and that these years are in fact the Age of the Democratic Revolution. . . ."

—R. R. PALMER

"While agreeing with Mr. Palmer's basic thesis and ends, I find it difficult to follow him all the way in his methods. . . ."

—ALFRED COBBAN

"Contemporaries and historians have not been mistaken in sensing and emphasizing the central importance of the French Revolution and its essential uniqueness. . . ."

—MARCEL REINHARD

II. The Eighteenth-Century Revolutions: Uniqueness and Interaction

England:
"The English Jacobins were essentially foreigners in their own country, isolated from the masses . . . ineffective as a political pressure group. . . ."

—R. C. COBB

Ireland:
"Like the French, the Irish revolutionaries would have toppled their ruling class, pursued a liberal . . . religious policy, confiscated the property of the absentee landlords. . . ."

—H. L. CALKIN

Austria:
"According to all the evidence available, the various activities which have gone into history as the Jacobin Conspiracy were little more than . . . an attempt to organize and coordinate the active opposition to the policies of Francis II's government. . . ."

—ERNST WANGERMANN

Holland:
"The Dutch Revolution of 1795 . . . reveals, on a small and well lit stage, a great many phenomena then common to western Europe and in some degree the Western world. . . ."

—R. R. PALMER

America:

"The danger here as elsewhere is that the historian, misled by his enthusiasm for the concept of 'revolution,' will posit too abrupt a set of changes, will pay too little attention to the evidences of historical continuity. . . ."

—Frederick B. Tolles

France and America:

"In preparing that collapse of France with its subsequent revolutionary ideology, the American revolution played a part that has not always been properly understood, though generally recognized. . . ."

—Louis Gottschalk

"The French Declaration of Rights is . . . concerned only with expressing a universal truth. The American Declarations of Rights . . . reflect the . . . language of the legal expert. . . . No two documents in this world are more dissimilar. . . ."

—Emile Boutmy

France:

". . . in the French Revolution, it is commonly said, the feudal order passed away and the rule of the bourgeoisie took its place. This is . . . the myth which has dominated serious research on the history of the French Revolution during the present century. . . ."

—Alfred Cobban

III. Perspectives on the Eighteenth Century

"The Anglo-Saxon revolutions had been directed against absolutism in behalf of a bourgeois-aristocratic alliance. . . . The real mission of the [French] Revolution was to be the revolution of equality. . . ."

—Georges Lefebvre

". . . the revolution became necessary because the government was incapable of undertaking the reforms carried out in other states. . . . yet basically the program involved was derived from enlightened absolutism. . . ."

—Martin Göhring

"I share the view that the revolutionary period has been studied too exclusively within a national framework. . . . In order to undertake comparative studies, a greater unity is needed. . . . We find such a unity in the concept of an occidental civilization. . . ."

—R. R. Palmer

"I . . . suggest that the great movement which overthrew the social, economic and political order of most of Europe and America between 1770 and 1849 should be described as "Western" or "Atlantic.". . . This is corroborated by an examination of the counterrevolution . . . [which] like the revolution itself, was also international and western. . . ."

—Jacques Godechot

PART I: THE PALMER THESIS: PRESENTATION AND CRITICISM

The World Revolution of the West: 1763–1801

R. R. PALMER

R. R. Palmer, professor of history at Princeton University, is one of the best known American authorities on eighteenth-century France. He has written widely respected books both on the pre-revolutionary "climate of opinion" and on the revolutionary government. His latest, widely acclaimed work, *The Age of the Democratic Revolution*, the first volume of which appeared in 1959, goes far beyond the usual national perspective to study the revolutionary events of the last forty years of the eighteenth century as an international phenomenon.

In the streets of Paris, on the ninth of Thermidor of the Year Six (July 27, 1798), there took place a long and memorable procession. It was in celebration of Liberty Day, as the anniversary of the fall of Robespierre was then officially called. It began at nine o'clock in the morning at the Museum of Natural History. First came cavalry and a band. They were followed by professors and students from the Museum, marching beside triumphal cars that bore various minerals, exotic plants, and some crystals presented by the people of Valais in Switzerland. There were also a live bear from the zoo at Berne, lions from Africa, and two camels and two dromedaries sent by General Bonaparte from Egypt. After more soldiers, and more musicians, came delegates from the printers of Paris, librarians of the public libraries, and professors from the *Polytechnique* and the *Collège de France*. Prize pupils from the new *école centrale* carried manuscripts and rare books. Next appeared teachers and students of the arts, who were followed by Art itself—the treasures captured by victorious armies in Italy: paintings by Titian, Raphael and Paul Veronese, sculpture in stupefying abundance, the Laocoön, the Dying Gladiator, the Discus Thrower and the Apollo Belvedere, to name only the most famous. Most conspicuous of all were the ancient bronze horses from St. Mark's in Venice. They bore an inscription: "Transported from Corinth to Rome, from Rome to Constantinople, from Constantinople to Venice, from Venice to France. They rest at last upon free ground." Numerous other inscriptions, up and down the procession, explained the assembled

From R. R. Palmer, "The World Revolution of the West," *Political Science Quarterly*, LXIX (1954), 1–14. Reprinted by permission of the *Political Science Quarterly*.

[In this and the following articles the footnote documentation has been omitted.]

wonders to onlookers. One was a quotation from Seneca: "To live ignorant is to be dead."

All this plunder, for such most of it literally was, was ceremoniously presented to the Minister of the Interior, who received it at the feet of a statue of liberty. The festivities ended with the ascension of a balloon, or "aerostat," carrying aloft more inscriptions, together with "attributes of liberty and the arts," and the tricolor of the Revolution.

The men in the French government who arranged this extraordinary spectacle obviously intended it to have a symbolic meaning. It may serve also as a symbol for us. It may remind us of certain paradoxes, or seeming paradoxes, of the French Revolution: the association of liberty with force, of enlightenment and education with propaganda and histrionics, of a sense of progress with a sense of conquest, of soldiers with professors, of a feeling of attachment to the Western tradition with one of angry repudiation of the historic past. And the bears, lions, camels, strange plants and imported statuary may suggest also the idea of a World Revolution, of which many people in Paris, and in other countries, believed France to be the center.

In the summer of 1798 France was bordered by other revolutionary republics in Holland, Switzerland and Italy. Belgium and the Rhineland had been annexed, and unrest spread through Germany. Ireland was in rebellion, and in Great Britain the government of William Pitt, to use the word of various British historians, was resorting to terror. In Sweden, said the British Foreign Secretary, half the people were Jacobins. In the United States, in July 1798, the same fear of Jacobins, that is of democrats, produced the Alien and Sedition laws; nor were such fears allayed when the democrats won the next election. The president of the college at Princeton, shortly thereafter, shuddered at "those irreligious and demoralizing principles which are tearing the bands of society asunder."

The idea that these events constituted a world revolution, that is, a revolution of the Western World, is a very old one, since it dates from the eighteenth century itself. Recently, both in this country and in Europe, historians have begun to revive it. I need only mention our own Louis Gottschalk, or Georges Lefebvre of the Sorbonne, who, rewriting in 1951 his book of 1930 on the French Revolution, completely recast it to show the supranational implications. It may be that we should try to develop some integrating or unifying conceptions for this whole revolutionary movement in Europe and America taken together. It is not enough to have a rough semi-Marxist idea of the "bourgeois revolution," or simply to place different countries side by side for comparison, or to speak vaguely of the "influence" of France or of America upon a world left otherwise undescribed.

Such a world revolution may be bounded, for convenience, by the dates 1763 and 1800 or 1801. At the hither end, we have a dramatic close in the election of Jefferson to the American presidency, and the personal triumph of Napoleon Bonaparte in Europe. The two events were not exactly alike, to be sure, but both were followed by a decline of political agitation. At the same time, with the Peace of Amiens and the Concordat both the British government and the papacy recognized the consequences of international revolutionary republicanism, at least tentatively and pending further developments.

There are good reasons for beginning about 1763. With the decade of the sixties some of the characteristics of the revolutionary era become apparent—the ideas and issues, the alignments of protagonists on both the domestic and the international fronts, the types of political activity and methods of rebellion against government, with the virtual creation of a public opinion on political questions in many countries. In the realm of ideas, the years 1762 and 1763 see the publication of the main writings of Rousseau, and we have it from Daniel Mornet, the leading authority, that the *philosophe* movement had triumphed by 1770. In 1765 the French Assembly of the Clergy issued its first wholesale condemnation of the *philosophe* literature, which it said would undermine, if unchecked, all churches, states and societies. The same years of the mid-sixties bring, in France, the quarrel of Louis XV's ministers with the more or less united *parlements* of the kingdom. The cry of "Wilkes and Liberty" is heard in England, and the Sugar Act and the Stamp Act arouse America. No one can read E. S. Morgan's new book, *The Stamp Act Crisis,* without sensing what was to come. He himself calls the American agitation of 1765 a revolution nipped in the bud. It anticipated what was soon to happen, in America and elsewhere, both in the ideas employed, that is, the appeal to historic or natural rights against a sovereign authority recognizing no direct dependence on the people, and in the practical tactics devised, that is, gatherings of the merchant and lawyer class into clubs and committees, and their exploiting of mob violence to obtain their ends. At the same time the close of the Seven Years' War marked the triumph of Great Britain and in particular of its Parliamentary governing class, the most brilliantly successful of all people under eighteenth-century conditions, and hence the least inclined to see conditions changed. The stage is already set for the solid British conservatism which was in time to be the main support of counterrevolution, and for that British superiority in wealth, and command of the sea, with the consequent anti-British feeling, which were to affect all international relations for many years.

The problem now is to suggest a few unifying themes, running through these years, and more or less common to an Atlantic civilization.

To begin with ideas. To imply that ideas "caused" the Revolution has long been the signal for controversy, carrying the implication of a conservative approach. Since the Revolution, and indeed before, as in the French Assembly of the Clergy of 1765, there have been warnings that the literature of the Enlightenment made people unruly and filled them with impractical ideas. This is probably true. It is not the whole truth, for the ideas in question were more than mere rebellious opinions. They derived from centuries of European thought, and they applied to the actual conditions of the day. The whole issue as between ideas and circumstances in the causation of the Revolution was set forth with extraordinary clarity, as early as 1799, by Friedrich Gentz. In 1790 a French conservative, Sénac de Meilhan, in his book of that year, remarked that "the French Revolution seems to be a revolution of the human mind."

The main idea, if we must single one out, seems to have been a demand for self-determination, a sense of autonomy of the personality, a refusal to accept norms laid down outside the self, leading sometimes to a profound subjectivity, or an insistence on self-expression rather than adjustment to preëxisting authoritative standards. This seems to be the message of Rousseau, in the *Confessions* and the novels as well as in the *Social Contract.* In the latter, it is a collective self that defines the right; and each citizen is triumphantly demonstrated to be subject and sovereign at the same time. The same note of personal autonomy underlies all the practical demands for liberty, political and economic. It may be found in Kant's metaphysics and in his political theory, and in the world-creating Ego of Fichte, who believed himself and his philosophy to be part and parcel of the revolutionary movement. It presumably explains what Hegel meant when he said that Mind became fully free only with the French Revolution. It inspired the educational doctrine of Pestalozzi, who welcomed the revolutionary Helvetic Republic in Switzerland. It has been found, by those versed in music, in the work of that obstreperous republican, Beethoven. It is obviously central to romanticism, and, in the demand for spontaneity and the rejection of artificial restraint, inspires the *Lyri-*

cal Ballads of 1798. Surely there exists here the opportunity for what modern parlance knows as a "synthesis," bringing together not only many peoples of different language or nationality, but also many different fields of activity and thought.

It might be shown also, in such a synthesis, how the universal impulse to liberty is at least in principle kept in order. Anarchic individualism is avoided, in the political sphere, by the stress on the equality of rights, and by the ideas of fraternity and of law; and all are bound together in the idea of constitutionalism. About fifteen new written constitutions were proclaimed in America, and ten in Europe, in the quarter-century ending in 1801. In economic theory, it is natural law, or the natural harmony, that prevents liberty from degenerating into confusion. In the arts, a generation that revived the sonnet can hardly be charged with looseness. In moral philosophy, with Rousseau and Kant, it is the human conscience that stands between freedom and anarchy. In more recent times, with the ideas of conscience and natural law losing their force, and the drive for emancipation or self-expression as strong as ever, a great deal of trouble has been attributed to such ideas. Some have sought philosophical composure in the Middle Ages. The matter cannot be amplified here. Suffice it to say that liberty has always been known to be dangerous.

A unified conception of world revolution would be the easier to arrive at if we could point to an organized and centrally directed revolutionary party, international in its operations. Conservatives in the 1790's, unable to believe that revolutionary sentiment had any real or, so to speak, legitimate foundation, naturally imagined that such an international conspiracy was at work. The French *émigré* Barruel, and the Scotsman John Robison, independently produced large treatises proving its existence. In this country Jedediah Morse spread the same alarm. There was, however, no such international organization. Agitators and subversives did exist in all countries, and sometimes French generals or civil commissioners in neighboring states employed secret agents. They had little or no connection with each other, or with the French government or any super-society in France. The French Jacobins were never secret, and had no organization after 1794. Revolutionary secret societies were more the consequence than the cause of the great revolution of the 1790's. The Italian Carbonari, for example, may be traced to a kind of Jacobin club in Burgundy in 1790. It was in a Paris prison, in 1795, that Babeuf launched the revolutionary underground of the nineteenth century. In 1798, when all England was reading the shocking revelations of Barruel and Robison, the House of Commons appointed a Committee of Secrecy to inquire into subversion. The committee made the strongest possible case to show a conspiratorial movement in England since 1792. It published numerous documents, and it named names. No French agent is mentioned in its report, and no foreigner other than Irish.

Class analysis offers another common theme. Carl Becker once observed of the American Revolution that, with the question of home rule settled by independence, it remained to be seen who should rule at home. Thus the establishment of independence was followed by the heightened democratic agitation of the 1790's. The same pattern can easily be seen in parts of Europe, especially in regions subject to a sovereignty increasingly felt to be foreign. Cases in point are the Lombard and Belgian provinces, under the Hapsburg emperor; or the Swiss territory of Vaud, which belonged to the canton of Berne. In Belgium the assertion of independence in 1789 was followed by the strife between Statists, the upper class of the old régime, which wanted no internal change, and the democratic or "Vonckist" party, which demanded new rights for the hitherto unprivileged classes. The same pattern can be traced even in countries having native governments, since under the old régime all governments were in a sense foreign to their populations, the lack of moral bond between ruler and ruled being precisely the point at issue. It is now generally agreed that, in France, the revolution began with a revolt of the nobility against royal absolutism. This was no mere prelude, but an integral phase of the movement. If this revolutionary rôle of the aristocracy is once fixed in mind, then the attempts of Polish gentry to stage a revolution against the partitioning Powers, or the uprising of Hungary against Joseph II, can be brought into a unified conception of a general revolution. Even in England some of the gentry favored parliamentary reform; and parliamentary reform, involving equal, individual, numerical and "real" representation in the House of Commons, was rightly felt by conservatives to be a revolutionary change, both in the vicious practice and in the virtuous theory of the British Constitution.

In most countries having a middle class a bourgeois phase soon followed the aristocratic protest, and the sub-bourgeois or working classes were often heard from also, not only in France, but in England, Scotland, Holland and elsewhere. A historian of the city of Manchester, for example, remarks that the United Englishmen of 1797 offered the first example in that city of working-class political organization without middle-class leadership or support. In the long run, however, the landed interest seems to have had the last word, and it was the action of country people, perhaps more than anything else, that determined what happened as between one place and another. Only in France and America did small farmers become really revolutionary, and only in these countries do we find complete and thoroughly indigenous revolutions. In Ireland the rural population was disaffected, but helpless. In England the "land" meant a well-contented aristocracy. In Eastern Europe the very ownership of rural land was generally confined to nobles, who were the only political class, so that there was scarcely a tremor of revolution except for the noble opposition to outside Powers. In the Kingdom of Naples, the flimsiness of the so-called Parthenopean Republic of 1799 was due to the nonparticipation of peasants; and Cardinal Ruffo, with his famous Army of the Holy Faith, easily won back the country, not by the forces of clericalism, but because, being the administrative type of churchman, he had constructive ideas on land reform and could appeal to peasants.

Class differences manifested themselves constitutionally, in almost every country affected by the revolution, in the question of whether the new state should be unitary or federal. In the Dutch provinces, the Swiss cantons, and the Italian republics, as in France after 1792, we hear the cry for a "republic one and indivisible." The same idea is evident in Belgium, in the German Rhineland and in Ireland with its United Irishmen, who believed that Irish Catholics and Presbyterians must combine indivisibly against the English. The idea of a republic "one and indivisible" was not primarily nationalist; at least, it had no necessary relation to linguistic or ethnic groups. It meant that persons struggling for a democratic revolution must integrate territorially for self-protection, since the old local units of province and town—Brittany and Languedoc, Bologna and Ferrara, Amsterdam and Rotterdam, Brabant and Flanders, Cologne and Mainz, not to mention the twenty-one boroughs of Cornwall—were everywhere the seats of entrenched, exclusive and self-perpetuating oligarchic or privileged families. To insist that these historically-developed corporate entities should retain a separate influence was called "federalism" in revolutionary parlance, and federalism was with reason regarded as one of the many aspects of counterrevolution. Advanced democrats everywhere demanded the dissolution of such entities into a uniform state built upon individual citizenship. It seems important to note that a contrary situation existed in America. The fact that Federalism in America meant the centralized state is a mere difference of words. The significant matter is that, in America, the advanced democrats continued to fear strong government, or any central government, and to put their trust in local authorities close to the people. In America it was the democrats who were "federalist" in the European sense. At a time when big government was even harder to keep under control than now, democracy in America was not committed to big government, as it had to be in Europe to exist at all. The difference is due, like so much else, to the fact that America had no old régime in the true European sense, and hence no such internecine struggle.

Finally, it is in the sphere of international relations, and especially in war, that a unifying conception for the era may be formed. It is the misfortune of our own generation to know something of the interaction between war and revolution, and we should perhaps therefore be able to analyze the corresponding phenomena of the eighteenth century with a dreary wisdom not given to Sorel or Von Sybel. Whether revolution must lead to war we cannot really be certain. It has been both affirmed and denied of the war of 1792. We do know that war can be a great breeder of revolution. We know, too, that war aims change during the stress of fighting; that governments or aroused peoples may crush enemies or seize and hold advantages in a way having little to do with initial ideology or intentions.

The revolutionary struggle, throughout the thirty-odd years, was inseparable from the struggle between England and France. The British government opposed every revolutionary effort—the American, the Irish, the Dutch of 1784 and the Belgian of 1789. It went to war with France in 1793 to maintain the *status quo* in Belgium and Holland, against which many Dutch and Belgians were in rebellion, but which for over a century had been favorable to British naval and mercantile interests. The French, on the other hand, under both the Bourbon and the ensuing republican governments, patronized virtually all revolutionary disturbances.

The French were the only people to make a lasting revolution by their own efforts. All others depended on them. The French shipped 30,000 muskets to America in the year 1777. Nine tenths of all the gunpowder used by Americans before the battle of Saratoga was from foreign sources, mainly French. It is clear that the success of the American revolt depended on France even before France openly intervened. In this respect the American Revolution resembles the revolutions twenty years later which produced the Batavian, Cisalpine and other short-lived republics. The difference lies in the fact that the French withdrew from America, leaving the country independent, whereas they did not, could not, or would not withdraw from Holland or Italy except by abandoning their supporters to the counterrevolution.

The fact that the French alone accomplished a revolution with their own resources leads to comparative reflections on the Reign of Terror. There is no simple explanation for the Jacobin Terror of 1793. There is therefore no simple explanation for its absence. Yet the fact is that only in France did revolutionaries not depend on outside aid, and that only France had a real Terror. The Americans in the 1770's, and in the 1790's the Dutch and the Italians, managed to conduct revolutions of some magnitude without going to such lengths as the French in 1793. One reason surely is that they did not depend on their own precarious revolutionary resources—unorganized, unreliable, shifting, opportunistic, and virtually ungovernable, as resources of men and material in time of revolution are. They expected and received the aid of France. As a working hypothesis, we may suppose that revolutionaries had three alternatives: either capitulation to the old régime, or terroristic control of the means of defiance, or the acceptance of outside aid. The French did not have the third alternative. Of others, including our own esteemed Founding Fathers, it may be argued that receipt of French aid spared them the unpleasant necessity of terrorizing their fellow countrymen more than they in fact did. The matter is at least worth considering.

It is clear that war aims changed with war itself. The British government under Pitt, late in 1792, declared that it had no interest in the internal government of France, and would go to war only to preserve the existing situation in Belgium and Holland. Within two years, in July 1794, the same Pitt, in a secret cabinet memorandum, was planning to let Austria keep its acquisitions while Great Britain retained all those "already or yet to be conquered in the East and West Indies." In five more years he doubted whether any lasting peace could be made except by restoring the French Bourbons—an opinion not shared by Prussia, Austria, or even the Bourbon monarchy of Spain.

The French went to war in 1792 in a spirit of crusading for liberty, of raising a world revolution against all kings and all nobles. As Brissot wrote, anticipating Lenin, "we cannot be at ease until all Europe is in flames." As the Abbé Grégoire put it, in a phrase that would have suited either Metternich or Franklin Roosevelt: "If my neighbor keeps a nest of vipers I have the right to stamp it out, lest I be its victim." But as early as 1793 a more national and hard-headed attitude began to prevail in France. There began to be a contemptuous feeling that no people except the French was really suited for liberty. The idea of world revolution gave way to the idea of revolution in one country first. Some writers, like Albert Mathiez, make a great deal of this change, which in a way relieved the Jacobins of responsibility for world turmoil. Actually the change made little practical difference. It is consequences, not intentions, that enter into the crude realm of fact. Since the enemies with whom they were at war were the privileged classes of Europe—the nobilities and town oligarchies and wealthy landowning clergy—the French republicans attacked them by attacking their sources of power, by abolishing their privileges, their laws, their tithes and their feudal rents, by summoning their former dependents to freedom, by granting equal rights to Jews, Protestants, Catholics, freethinkers or whoever it might be that was outside the locally established church—and even by the confiscation of property, the property of hostile ruling classes, be it understood. Such procedure horrified conservatives, especially in England, where it was ascribed to some peculiar perversity in the Jacobin character, or to an excessive belief in abstract ideas. It was not altogether different from what happened to the South during and after our Civil War, or from what governments in general seem historically to have done in pursuing conquest or suppressing opposition. One thinks of the Celtic regions of the British Isles, and the Scottish Highlands as recently as 1745.

The point is that revolution does not have to be caused by revolutionary ideas. It may only be a weapon of war. The distinction is never clear. In France, even under the consulate and empire, there were many who remained attached to revolutionary ideas. They believed in principle in liberating men from feudalism, clericalism or stupidity. Outside of France there were idealistic persons who first welcomed the French, then turned against them, disillusioned. The fact that they turned anti-French does not mean that in all cases they turned against revolutionary ideas, since the revolution was not French alone. They became the spiritual or actual fathers of the European revolutionaries of 1830 or 1840. The case of Michael Venedey is an example. He was a German republican of 1797, his son was a German republican of 1848.

Or again, if we say that revolution need not be caused by revolutionary ideology, we may have in mind that societies collapse for negative reasons, not so much from the strength of revolutionary sentiment as from the absence of any powerful sentiment in favor of the existing order. There were important revolutionary elements in Holland, Belgium, the Rhineland, Switzerland and Italy; but what caused the collapse of old governments and governing classes, in every one of these countries, was the war. More specifically, it was that they would not or could not defend themselves, that their own peoples did not believe in them, that there was no loyalty, faith or conviction on which to build, that they all were permeated by neutralism, and hoped plaintively, and vaguely, to be rescued by British money or the British fleet. In Holland in 1794 the Prince of Orange attempted a levy in mass; he is said to have raised fifty men. In Belgium the authorities were afraid to arm the people. In Italy it had long been unheard of for Italians to be soldiers. The Swiss had not fought in their own cause for generations. All fell before revolutionary republicanism, French and domestic.

The French, being at war, accepted assistance wherever offered. They stirred up the very dregs of society, as we may read in a hundred contemporary accusations. They brought the "masses," or at least a great many lower-middle-class and working people, into the practical politics of the Western World. By a historical irony, the liberal bourgeois awakened his Marxist doom. As for the British, being also at war, they brought into the practical politics of the Western World, though it would be premature to call it a Marxist doom, the mammoth power of Imperial Russia. No doubt historical irony can be overdone. Yet as early as 1775 there was talk in England of using Russian mercenaries in America. The Earl of Suffolk jocosely remarked that 20,000 Russians would be "charming visitors to New York and would civilize that part of America." Vergennes, alarmed, foresaw that Britain might some day hire Russian troops for operations in Western Europe. In 1796 the British Cabinet agreed to give the island of Corsica to Russia. In 1798 Henry Dundas advised his cabinet colleague, Pitt, to "subsidize an army of Russians for British purposes," to attack Holland, defend Switzerland, capture Malta, open the markets of South America, or occupy Brest. In 1799 there was talk of using Russians in Ireland. In that same year Vergennes' fears were realized when Russian troops, paid for by Great Britain, invaded Switzerland and Holland, on their way to France. It seems strangely modern to find Reubell, the former Director, declaring in 1801 that his policy of revolutionizing Switzerland in 1798 had prevented the Cossacks from riding into Paris.

The age of the French Revolution, it may be said in closing, has been used historically for a great many purposes. It has been used to explain the rise of nationalism or of liberalism, of class struggle or the "perpetual revolution" of Trotsky, to celebrate the freedom of thought, or, contrariwise, to demonstrate that dogmatic Jacobin ideology must lead to totalitarianism. Let us avail ourselves of the privilege of our predecessors, and use the revolutionary era to investigate what is most on our minds, to find out what a world is like that is divided by revolution and war. There is something to be said for leaving the national histories of France, or Italy, or Holland, to persons born or living in those countries. Perhaps we in America are best equipped to be the synthesizers. As that notable revolutionary, Thomas Paine, remarked in a notable revolutionary year, 1776, America is "the colony of all Europe." We are of all European nationalities, and of none; and so should be the better able to see the whole movement as one common to the Atlantic world. If we do, we shall not be mere innovators, nor be forcing the past to fit the present. We shall be saying what contemporaries before 1800 all but universally believed. We shall be performing the oldest and humblest of all the rôles assigned to history—the preservation of memory. Indeed, I am reminded of the very first words of the first book of Herodotus, where he says that the aim of his "researches," as he calls them, is that the memory of the past may not be blotted out by time, that the actions of Greeks and barbarians may be known, "and especially that the causes may be remembered for which they waged war with each other." Each can decide for himself which were the Greeks, and which the barbarians. Or he may think that it was really a civil war in Hellas.

The Age of the Democratic Revolution

R. R. PALMER

The present work attempts to deal with Western Civilization as a whole, at a critical moment in its history, or with what has sometimes recently been called the Atlantic Civilization, a term probably closer to reality in the eighteenth century than in the twentieth. It is argued that this whole civilization was swept in the last four decades of the eighteenth century by a single revolutionary movement, which manifested itself in different ways and with varying success in different countries, yet in all of them showed similar objectives and principles. It is held that this forty-year movement was essentially "democratic," and that these years are in fact the Age of the Democratic Revolution. "Democratic" is here to be understood in a general but clear enough sense. It was not primarily the sense of a later day in which universality of the suffrage became a chief criterion of democracy, nor yet that other and uncertain sense, also of a later day, in which both Soviet and Western-type states could call themselves democratic. In one way, it signified a new feeling for a kind of equality, or at least a discomfort with older forms of social stratification and formal rank. . . . Politically, the eighteenth-century movement was against the possession of government, or any public power, by any established, privileged, closed, or self-recruiting groups of men. It denied that any person could exercise coercive authority simply by his own right, or by right of his status, or by right of "history," either in the old-fashioned sense of custom and inheritance, or in any newer dialectical sense, unknown to the eighteenth century, in which "history" might be supposed to give some special elite or revolutionary vanguard a right to rule. The "democratic revolution" emphasized the delegation of authority and the removability of officials, precisely because, as we shall see, neither delegation nor removability were much recognized in actual institutions.

It is a corollary of these ideas that the American and the French Revolutions, the two chief actual revolutions of the period, with all due allowance for the great differences between them, nevertheless shared a good deal in common, and that what they shared was shared also at the same time by various people and movements in other countries, notably in England, Ireland, Holland, Belgium, Switzerland and Italy, but also in Germany, Hungary, and Poland, and by scattered individuals in places like Spain and Russia. . . .

Even if there was a general revolutionary disturbance between about 1760 and about 1800, it does not follow, without further explanation, that "democratic" is the best word to describe it. It is well known that Thomas Jefferson did not much favor the use of the word; and we often read, at least in American books, that the term in the 1790's became an epithet or smear-word, by which persons were designated against their will, and usually

From R. R. Palmer, *The Age of the Democratic Revolution,* Vol. I (Princeton, 1959), pp. 4–20. Reprinted by permission of Princeton University Press.

falsely, like persons falsely called communists at a later day. The belief that the word had no willing acceptance in the eighteenth century actually plays into the hands of the modern Left; thus a Dutch scholar has argued, partly on the mistaken ground that "democracy" was little heard in Holland before 1800, that the modern "Eastern" use of the word, implying an economic rather than a political equality, and dating from the rise of social democracy in the 1880's, is historically more legitimate than the modern "Western" use. The fact seems to be that "democracy" and "democrat" enjoyed more currency before 1800 than is commonly supposed. It must be remembered that the words "liberal," "radical," and "progressive" did not exist. When moderates or conservatives wished to indicate the dangerous drift of the times, or when the more advanced spirits spoke of themselves, they might very well use the words "democrat" or "democracy." . . .

The two nouns, "democrat" and "aristocrat," were coinages of the period, unknown before the 1780's. No "democrats" fought in the American Revolution; and the Age of Aristocracy, as long as it was unchallenged, heard nothing of "aristocrats." Neither word was current in English before 1789; in France *aristocrate* crops up in the reign of Louis XVI, *démocrate* not until 1789. It may be that the words were first coined by the Dutch. It seems certain, in any case, that their first currency was in the Low Countries, in the Dutch revolution of 1784–1787 and the Belgian revolution of 1789–1791. We find *aristocraten* used by Dutch burghers as early as 1784. The Rotterdam patrician, van Hogendorp, writing in the French language in 1786, declares that his country is troubled by a cabal. "People say," he adds, "that this cabal is divided into aristocrats and democrats." "Aristocrat" entered into popular parlance among the Dutch in these years; but "democrat" remained rare, the popular party calling itself Patriot. In Belgium, however, that is, the Austrian Netherlands, in the revolt of 1789 against the emperor, the advanced party came to call itself Democrat. By January 1791 its leaders were speaking of *les braves Démocrates* and *les bons Démocrates*. One even wrote, *"Vive la Démocratie!"* . . .

"Democrat" was rarely used in France, despite its currency in Belgium in 1790 and 1791. It was probably coined, in France as in Holland or Belgium, in contradistinction to "aristocrat." Ferdinand Brunot, in his tremendous history of the French language, lists two hundred and six nouns and phrases designating political alignments during the Revolution. "Democrat" is in the list, but there are many more familiar terms, such as "patriots," "Jacobins," or "sansculottes." Dubois-Crancé, the future regicide, used it in 1790 in speaking on the military policy suitable to the new France. He describes the citizen soldier—"a patriot, an honest democrat." In 1791 Brissot claimed to advocate "a popular monarchy, tending to the popular side. Such is my democracy." In 1793, when Louis XVI was executed, the drums rolled to smother the last sounds and the crowds shouted *"Vive la République!"* One young man heard, or at least reported, "Long live Democracy!" He was, however, a Greek, writing to a fellow countryman in the Greek language. It may be that "democracy" to him, not being a foreign word, could convey a feeling that it lacked for western Europeans; that he used it naturally as a translation for the Latin "republic," to express the ideals and passions that he sensed in revolutionary Paris.

With the advent of the Jacobins and the Terror, "democracy" became more frequent, though never common. It was occasionally used at the Jacobin Club, where Camille Desmoulins cried that "the English people must be exterminated from Europe, unless they democratize themselves!" Hérault-Séchelles, submitting what is called the Jacobin constitution to the Convention for adoption, praised it as "representative and democratic." The constitution itself, though in fact democratic, allowing universal male suffrage and providing measures of initiative and referendum, does not use the word. . . .

In Holland after 1795 there was an important newspaper at Amsterdam called *De Democraten*. The Amsterdam political club said it wanted the *democratisch systema*. Even the French Directory, which used the word sparingly, declared in instructions for its agent in Holland, in December 1797, that the Dutch people desired a "free and democratic constitution." About a third of the members of the Dutch constituent assembly signed a petition, in January 1798, in favor of "a democratic representative constitution." A constitutional committee, in February, affirmed to the French agent, Delacroix, that the Dutch were "capable of a greater measure of democracy than would be suitable for the French."

In parts of Germany, notably the Rhenish states, there were people whose ideas were in effect democratic, but they seem to have used the word less often than the Dutch. One clubroom, in 1792, is reported to have had a sign on its wall reading *Vive la Démocratie. Au diable les aristocrates!* —in French! The journalist Lange, in an article comparing aristocracy and democracy, boldly declared for the latter, which, he said, offered more freedom to the real inequalities of human talent. . . .

In Switzerland, the constitution of the Helvetic Republic, which was proclaimed by the French in 1798, declared in its Article II that "the form of government, whatever modifications it may undergo, shall at all times be a representative democracy." Of all the written constitutions promulgated in Europe and America, in the last quarter of the eighteenth century, this is apparently the only one to call itself explicitly democratic. Its author was the Basel revolutionary, Peter Ochs, who spent a good deal of time in Paris. . . .

It was in Italy that the word "democracy," in a favorable sense, was most commonly used in the years from 1796 to 1799. The most striking example comes from no less a person than Pius VII, two years before his elevation to the papacy. From 1785 to 1800 he was Bishop of Imola, a town in the northern part of the Papal States. Revolutionary disturbances broke out on every side when the French army, under Bonaparte, conquered Lombardy in 1796. Imola was absorbed into the Cisalpine Republic. On Christmas Eve 1797 the Bishop of Imola issued a Christmas homily to his diocese. It contains the word "democracy" eleven times within the space of a few hundred words. "The form of democratic government adopted among us, most beloved brethren," he said, "is not inconsistent with the Gospel . . ."

The Milan popular club announces: *"facciamo uno governo democratico."* People shout: *"La Democrazia o la Morte!"* Others wish to "democratize the People," to create "a democratic base." A newspaper declares that any republic in Italy must be "a democracy, one and indivisible." Pamphlets are entitled "Resurgence of oppressed democracy" and "Democratic education for the Italian people." At Venice there is talk of creating a democracy, and Democratic Fecundity is exhibited by an engaged couple marching in a procession. At Rome a man named Martelli speaks casually of what will happen after the "democratization" of Naples and Tuscany. A proclamation reads, "Form yourselves into a democracy, People of the Roman Republic." There is a theatrical production called "The Democratization of Heaven." There is a grand ball in honor of Bonaparte: no "ladies" and very few *seigneurs romains* were present, but this is not surprising, because "the party was democratic." And with republican Rome facing attack in 1799 by the King of Naples, the leaders try, though in vain, to make it a war for "democracy." . . .

In England and Scotland the antidemocrats seem to have monopolized the word. Wordsworth did indeed say in a private letter in 1794: "I am of that odious class of men called democrats." But he said it with a note of defiance which eloquently suggests the disrepute of the word. Even

Thomas Paine rarely employs it, but in the third chapter of *The Rights of Man,* Part Two, he does address himself to the meaning of "republic," "aristocracy," and "democracy." "Democracy" occurs eleven times within about five hundred words. He distinguishes it from direct or "simple" democracy. "Retaining, then, Democracy as the ground, and rejecting the corrupt systems of Monarchy and Aristocracy, the representative system naturally presents itself. . . . It is on this system that the American Government is founded. It is representation ingrafted upon Democracy." There are only three texts of the period, to my knowledge, where the author uses "democracy" in a favorable sense, as often as eleven times within a few hundred words; and these three texts are those of Paine, Robespierre, and the man who became Pius VII.

In the United States, where the people were still in large measure culturally British, and in particular among those of the educated classes, there was undoubtedly some hesitation by democrats to adopt the word "democratic." . . . James Monroe, after reading the Anglo-Franco-American Paine's *Rights of Man,* remarks in a letter to Jefferson, in 1791, that he agrees with the author, and that "the bulk of the [American] people are for democracy." In the following years a great many political clubs, not unlike the radical societies of Britain and Continental Europe, began to appear in various parts of the United States. . . . The third to be organized, and the first to adopt the name "democratic," was the Democratic Society of Pennsylvania. Its members at first planned to use the name Sons of Liberty; it was the French minister, Genêt, who suggested the word "democratic" for this purpose. Sixteen others soon thereafter put "democratic" in their titles. . . .

It is, therefore, no anachronism to apply the word "democratic" to the eighteenth-century revolution. It was the last decade of the century that brought the word out of the study and into actual politics. . . .

The Age of the Democratic Revolution

ALFRED COBBAN

Alfred Cobban, professor of French history at University College, London, and editor of the scholarly journal, *History*, is the most eminent living British historian of France. His many publications have ranged from eighteenth-century political theory, diplomacy, and public opinion to considerations of the problems of modern nationalism and dictatorship. Most recently, Professor Cobban has published an excellent two-volume *History of Modern France*.

THERE has recently been a tendency among modern historians to pay increased attention to the movements which transcend national boundaries. Thus the revolutionary wave which swept one country after another in the latter years of the eighteenth century is now seen as in some respects the inroads of a single great tide. To write the history of such a movement is a difficult task. A mastery of the available literature in various languages, the basic research necessary to explore at least a few of the crucial gaps in our knowledge, a fundamental re-thinking of the political developments and an exploration of the social structure out of which they arise, are all necessary. The courage of Professor R. R. Palmer of Princeton University in launching on this colossal enterprise deserves all the more admiration. Where other historians have ventured only to suggest international influence and affiliations, he has attempted for the first time a connected history based on an integrated pattern.

The Age of the Democratic Revolution: a Political History of Europe and America, 1760–1800: Volume I, *The Challenge,* is even more than this. With greater frankness than many other historians, who also have their prejudices, exhibit, Professor Palmer in writing of the struggle as one between (using the terms broadly) the aristocratic and the democratic conceptions of the community, asserts his own predilection for American democracy as against the inequalities of the European monarchical and aristocratic systems. He also divorces the eighteenth-century democratic from the modern Marxist revolution, writing, "It is permitted to believe that a better society, more humane, more open, more flexible, more susceptible to improvement, more favorable to physical welfare and to the pursuit of higher concerns, issued from the democratic revolution of the eighteenth century than from the communist revolution of the twentieth." At the same time he insists that the eighteenth century did indeed witness a revolution. To the European reader his argument that "opposition to one revolution is no reason for rejecting all revolutions" may seem superfluous; but he reminds us that "there was something in the atmosphere of 1955 . . . which made it important, for some, to dissociate

From Alfred Cobban, "The Age of the Democratic Revolution," *History,* XLV (London: 1960), 234–239. Reprinted by permission of the author and *History*.

the American Revolution from other revolutions." Admittedly, in present-day historical writing "there is no agreement on what the American Revolution was"; and he tells us that "those who discount the revolutionary character of the American Revolution seem to be gaining ground." Against this, he presents an interpretation of the American War of Independence "on the analogy of revolutions in Europe." This is an interesting and profitable parallel, though Mr. Palmer possibly carries it a little too far. What happened in America, he suggests, was even more revolutionary than what happened subsequently in France, tested by two "quantitative and objective measures": first, the percentage of those who fled from the colonies as loyalists, which was 2.4, whereas the percentage of *émigrés* was only 0.5, in relation to the whole population; secondly, the compensation paid to the *émigrés* in 1825, which was only twelve times as large as that paid earlier by the British government to the loyalists though revolutionary France was ten times as large as revolutionary America. It would be easy to play this game with other sets of figures, but we shall have no difficulty in agreeing that the American was a real revolution without going into perhaps not very convincing statistical comparisons.

On America Mr. Palmer seems to rely on the most recent historical work. On France he faithfully follows the interpretation of Lefebvre, and if this is to be quarrelled with it can be only on the basis of new research. On Great Britain his step seems unsure. At the very beginning he tells us, in a footnote, "It will be evident to the alert reader that I do not share the revisionist admiration shown by L. B. Namier for the old House of Commons." No historian is obliged to share all the views of Sir Lewis; I do not myself. But it might have been preferable not to dismiss the work of the leading historian of the period in a single footnote, even if it represents a tendency with which Mr. Palmer does not sympathize and if its interpretation of British politics runs counter to his own. One historian cannot, of course, be equally familiar with the history of all countries, and the analysis of British developments here sometimes suggests a subject "got up" for the occasion but not really understood.

The importance of occasional confused statements should, however, not be exaggerated. On Mr. Palmer's history of the political developments in Sweden, Russia, Poland, Bohemia, Hungary, the Austrian Netherlands, the Swiss Cantons and so on, it would need as many different historians to comment adequately. Since he is writing on a broad scale it is almost inevitable that there will be statements that a historian with more detailed knowledge would want to modify or delete. But this does not affect the validity of his thesis of a single great democratic revolution dominating this period, or diminish his belief in the value of that revolution. In both respects I would go a long way with him. I think there was such a revolution, and when the ideals of the revolutionaries are compared with the facts of the various social and political systems against which they were revolting, my sympathies are certainly with them.

On the other hand, while agreeing with Mr. Palmer's basic thesis and ends, I find it difficult to follow him all the way in his methods. He makes extensive use of parallels, which seem to me sometimes rather far-fetched. To fit Great Britain into the pattern, George III's political activities are likened to those of Louis XV, Maria Theresa and Gustavus III. With Pitt in office he finds that "as in the days of the Stamp Act, there was a remote and ludicrous English analogy to the enlightened despotism of the Continent, which the Whiggish traditions of English history have perhaps concealed." The British House of Commons is compared with the parlement of Grenoble because it had a large proportion of young members in its ranks. Pitt's reform bill of 1785 is likened to the Maupeou reforms in France. Burke is "an eloquent writer, a man of feeling, and an expatriate, in many ways surprisingly like Jean-Jacques Rousseau." When France, Zurich and Bern employ their treaty rights to intervene in Geneva, there is "a premonition of the Holy Alliance and the Protocol of Troppau." Admitting a difference in scale and intensity, this time I think on the side of France, Mr. Palmer finds the France of the Reign of Terror foreshadowed in detail by the America of 1776—a revolutionary government, committees of public safety, representatives on mission, paper money and forged paper money, price controls, oaths, delation, confiscations, Jacobins who wind up as sober guardians of the law—"how much it all suggests what was to happen in France a few years later!" It seems to me that to push the parallel into such detail is to weaken rather than strengthen the case.

When Mr. Palmer finds, on the contrary, a parallel which runs counter to his own ideas, he has no difficulty in detecting differences. Thus his most prominent theme is that of an aristocratic counter-revolution, accompanying, following or even preceding the democratic revolution. He sees it in France, Great Britain and Ireland, Geneva, the Dutch Republic, Russia, Sweden, Poland, Prussia. Some American historians have also seen a kind of "aristocratic resurgence" in the United States after independence, but Mr. Palmer patriotically protests, "My own view is that, while a new upper class was undoubtedly growing up in the United States, it was clearly more dynamic, more oriented to the future, more receptive to change than the aristocracies of Europe." Elsewhere he tends to subordinate the differences to the similarities. His approach is well represented by what he writes of the French Revolution: "So much being said for the uniqueness of the French Revolution, the pattern used in foregoing chapters will be applied to it in the following pages." Since, I suspect, the pattern was originally derived from a study of the French Revolution, it naturally fits very well in this case.

Another danger involved in his method is the temptation unconsciously to omit those facts that do not fit the pattern. Thus we are told that the aristocratic parties in the smaller countries "showed a strong tendency to depend on foreign aid." This is true, but the fact that so also did their democratic opponents, though not ignored, emerges rather less emphatically. We are also told that "the leaders of democratization showed an affinity for France" as against Great Britain. Indeed they did in America and the Dutch Republic. But why omit to say that in Geneva it was the oligarchy who called in France and their opponents who looked to Britain? It is mentioned that among the Genevan democrats Clavière settled in France, but at first, like most of the leaders of the Genevan movement, he fled to England and obtained financial aid from the British Government. It is true, as Mr. Palmer observes, that "not everything can be told." Perhaps the Corsican struggle for independence, which also looked to Great Britain, is not relevant to his thesis. But in discussing enlightened despotism, why Sweden and Russia, and not Spain, Naples or Denmark? In the case of Spain it is frankly admitted that material to support the main thesis cannot be extracted from its history. Moving closer home, Mr. Palmer speaks of the "rough kind of equality" in the colonies. Twice he adds, except for slavery, but are two perfunctory references enough for such a prominent feature of the American scene?

This raises a further difficulty. No doubt it could be argued that slavery, and other matters that are omitted, are irrelevant to the argument. And obviously if we allowed exceptions to dictate our interpretations we should never be able to detect any general tendencies in history at all. Mr. Palmer has made a gallant attempt to break away from the concentration on individual trees which during the last generation seems to have made it impossible for many historians ever to recognize a wood. If a major and essential aspect of a subject were to be excluded, that would be a different matter, and unfortunately I cannot help feeling that this is what has happened here. Since Mr. Palmer entitles his book a "Political History" it would be grossly unfair to criticize it simply on the ground that it is not something else. The problem is whether the democratic revolutions of which he writes can be understood in purely, or even predominantly, political terms. Thus he seems, in writing of the French Revolution, to want to draw a distinction between the revolution, which was political, and its results which might be social. He says, "It remained primarily political . . . But in its effects on society and social and moral attitudes, it went far beyond the merely political." I wonder if this is a possible distinction. And if the results of the democratic movement extend far beyond the political, do not also its causes? One can see the difficulty: the material for a synthesis on social evolution in the second half of the eighteenth century hardly exists. Lacking this, a general history has to be political or nothing. Where some serious work has been done on social analysis, as it has in the history of America, Mr. Palmer does in fact make good use of it. This may be why his discussion of the American Revolution seems so much more substantial than what he has to say of the democratic revolution in other countries. It may also be the reason why the American Revolution is the one which, in his picture, breaks away farthest from the generalized pattern.

There is another aspect of the democratic revolution which also still lacks fundamental research. This is the development of the idea of popular sovereignty and its progress from theory to practice. Mr. Palmer curiously (but inevitably, given the present state of work on the subject) devotes far more space to aristocratic than to democratic theory. The latter seems to boil down to Rousseau's *Contrat social,* "the great book of the political revolution." This is a subject for endless controversy, which need not be explored here; but Mr. Palmer weakens the case when he tells us that Sieyès "translated the ideas of the *Contrat social* into the language of 1789." The opposition between *Qu'est-ce que le Tiers Etat?* and the *Contrat social* is glaring, and if Sieyès adequately represented the ideas of the Tiers Etat of 1789, the political influence of the *Contrat social* on them must have been negligible. But the history of the political ideas of the period requires much further investigation.

If we end on a series of questions, this should not diminish our gratitude to Professor Palmer for being the first to venture on the bold synthesis which forces them upon our attention. We are beginning to have some idea who and what the American revolutionaries were. But who were the Dutch Patriots? What kind of merchants were these who are said to have rioted in the streets of Amsterdam, and what was the "amorphous populace" that shouted *Oranje boven!* through The Hague? Because of the valuable work of Susanne Tassier we know about some of the Vonckist democrats in the Austrian Netherlands, whose leaders at least seem to have been largely professional men, but the social composition of the French revolutionaries of 1789, and how far they can be called democrats, is evidently still a matter of controversy.

Since Mr. Palmer throughout his book emphasizes that the democrats in America, Holland, Geneva and elsewhere looked to France, one might have expected to learn something of the democratic movements before 1789 inside France itself. Instead we are taken straight from the Aristocratic Revolt to the "revolutionary psychology" of 1789, and whether this is to be regarded as essentially democratic is not clear to me, though at the end of the book, in an Appendix, it is argued that the Constitution of 1791 was "somewhat more 'democratic,' and somewhat less 'bourgeois,' than has been commonly said." More than this is needed if the democratic revolution in France, when it comes, is not to be produced, surprisingly but unconvincingly, like the card one originally thought of, out of the conjurer's pack. Mr. Palmer does indeed tell us that "France before 1789 was full of Dutch, Belgian, Swiss, Irish, and even English political expatriates." I can't identify any English or Irish political refugees at this time, but that may be mere ignorance. The point is, that for a French democratic revolution it would be useful to have some Frenchmen. I am not suggesting that antecedents of 1793 and 1794 might not be found in France if they were looked for, but only that until they have been looked for there is a fatal gap in Mr. Palmer's thesis.

Again, whether the reformers in England were democrats in Mr. Palmer's sense of the term, and whether the English Protestant dissenters and the Irish Catholics fall into the same category, if 1780 in the British Isles was indeed a French Revolution *manqué,* what roots there were, in towns like Sheffield and Bristol before the 'nineties, for the later growth of the Corresponding Societies—these are questions which it is easier to ask than answer. What do we know of democracy in Sweden, or Poland, or Austria? It is no criticism of Mr. Palmer to say that his book does not answer these questions, for the research has not been done that would enable them, and many others like them, to be answered. Really his "Age of the Democratic Revolution," which used to be called the Age of Enlightened Despotism, could, on the strength of his analysis, with much more appropriateness be called the Age of the Aristocratic Revival, for this is the subject to which the greater part of his book is devoted. It is far better documented (outside America) than the democratic movement, but is this because it was a much more widespread and substantial movement, or merely because we lack the knowledge of the democratic movement that would reveal its real shape to us? The function of the historian is not necessarily to answer all questions. One sign of a good history is that it should incite us to ask them. This Mr. Palmer's *Age of the Democratic Revolution* does in ample measure.

Historical Perspectives of the French Revolution

MARCEL REINHARD

Marcel Reinhard, professor of history at the Sorbonne in Paris and director of the Institute for Revolutionary History, has achieved prominence both as historian of the French Revolution and as a pioneer in the history of population. He is best known for a brilliant two-volume biography of the revolutionary "Organizer of Victory," Lazare Carnot. Professor Reinhard tends to represent a more exclusively national approach to revolution than most of the other historians included in this volume.

Was there a French Revolution or a revolution in France? Such are the terms in which this question has been raised by my friend and colleague J. Godechot and by R. Palmer. . . . Should we drop the bad habit of speaking of a French Revolution in the same narrow way that such classical historians as Pierre Michelet and Tocqueville did? This is indeed what J. Godechot asks us to do. Rather, he suggests, we should consider a great Atlantic revolution, composed of a series of revolutions which began in 1763 in the English colonies of America, thence spreading to Switzerland, the Netherlands, Ireland, France, Germany, back to Switzerland, to Italy, even to the eastern Mediterranean, to Egypt, and to Spanish America. In the light of such a perspective, the French phenomenon can be viewed simply as one link in a chain. Is Mr. Palmer perhaps a little less dogmatic? Mr. Palmer warns against temptations that have led historians of different national backgrounds to exaggerate the revolutionary spirit of their compatriots before 1800, while underestimating the influence of the French Revolution. Even so, both Palmer and Godechot underline the features which are common to all these revolutionary movements. They share a similar ideology, exalting liberty and equality; they affirm popular sovereignty and self-determination; they stress the similarity in organization, in tactics, and revolutionary tasks, which in turn leads to a similar conclusion: the triumph of liberalism, nationalism, and the bourgeoisie. It seems to us that this thesis distorts true perspective by overemphasizing common denominators and by underrating the substantial differences in scope and revolutionary content of all these movements. Contemporaries and historians have not been mistaken in sensing and emphasizing the central importance of the French Revolution and its essential uniqueness, to such a degree that the very word "revolution" underwent a change in meaning and became associated with events in France in the late eighteenth century. It is quite true that at the beginning of the French Revolution the American example was cited, and that

From Marcel Reinhard, "Travaux et perspectives sur la Révolution française," *Annales—Economies, Sociétés, Civilisations*, XIV (1959), 553–557. Reprinted by permission of *Annales*. Translated by the Editor.

during the same first few months some Englishmen, Frenchmen, and Germans were convinced that France was following in the footsteps of England. This was a short-lived delusion.

In its development the French Revolution disconcerted, alienated, and antagonized the majority of those who had supported the English, American, Dutch, and Belgian revolutionary movements. Even those who continued to embrace Paine and Bentham were bypassed by events in France. As the French Revolution became increasingly radical, increasingly revolutionary, increasingly violent, the early phase that had horrified Burke had receded into the past. The French Revolution was not a revolution of the Anglo-Saxon type, but a uniquely French phenomenon, though in reflecting the expansive tendencies of the *Grande Nation* this revolution did have universal overtones.

In the course of our comparative studies of the principles and origins of the various declarations of the rights of man, we have lost sight of the fact that the French declaration was contingent upon the French *ancien régime:* the French institutional setting alone can explain the French declaration of the rights of man; indeed, this declaration was conceived in order to overthrow the institutional framework.

Unquestionably this declaration also had its ideological side. This ideological content was not exclusively French, despite the dominant influence of the French *philosophes* whose doctrines had been exported to the United States before re-entering France. When all is said and done, however, the declaration served above all as a war machine against French absolutism, inequality in every domain . . . and the intolerance of Roman Catholicism. It must be reiterated that this declaration, formulated at the very beginning of the revolution, was more daring, more explosive, more revolutionary in France than its counterpart in America. In France the tug-of-war between principles and institutions—the declaration and the existing social structure—was clearly far greater and more violent. The French *ancien régime* was mirrored in a social structure differing from that of other countries. Basically, the French declaration and its evolution, as well as the simultaneous political activity, can be explained by the French aristocratic reaction which created a much more revolutionary situation than existed elsewhere.

The declaration served as an arsenal from which arguments on behalf of ever more daring proposals were drawn, justifying ever more revolutionary acts. This is borne out by a comparison of the successive declarations of rights—proposed or adopted—and the successive constitutions: each was increasingly democratic, popular, and egalitarian. At least till the time of Thermidor the tidal wave which swept away the reservations and ambiguities of its beginnings demonstrated the radicalism and uniqueness of the French Revolution. This revolution had been accentuated by internal and external resistance, by the ruses and the threats of its adversaries. The unique scope and force of counterrevolutionary resistance explains why revolution elsewhere was less complete in its ideology as well as in its impact upon the economy, religion, army, and warfare. Danton took over where Lafayette left off; Robespierre and Saint-Just overtook and crushed Danton; Babeuf and his supporters proclaimed the social revolution that even went beyond what the Mountain had advocated. Abroad, while the revolution was looked upon as an inspiring example by some men, others agitated for a crusade against this monster. All agreed, however, that this was a levelling and victorious revolution the like of which could only have originated in France, and that could only have emanated from France. For a long time thereafter the fierce stanzas of the *Marseillaise* still conjured up the fearful revolutionary image. The revolution was indeed French.

While abroad men had aimed for the freedom of the individual and for national self-determination, in France equality loomed more important: "Not liberty but equality made the revolution." Napoleon was to repeat this phrase of Mirabeau's which defines the very Frenchness of the revolution.

This singularity was derived from the very essence of the French nation: from its public opinion, its economy, and society. The uniqueness of this French phenomenon may be ascribed on one hand to aristocratic resistance, on the other hand to the revolutionary energy of the Third Estate. The Godechot-Palmer thesis does suggest a careful study of the economy and society of the various revolutionary nations, in order to compare them to the French setting. Only in this way will it be possible to make a proper evaluation of similarities and differences. If this is done, this thesis will at least be of some value, such as the comparisons between the achievements of the French Revolution and the enlightened despots that were once current.

PART II: THE EIGHTEENTH–CENTURY REVOLUTIONS: UNIQUENESS AND INTERACTION

The English Jacobins and the French Revolution

R. C. COBB

R. C. Cobb, a British historian of the University College of Wales and of Manchester, is well known among specialists on the French Revolution. Most of his work has appeared in the form of articles in French scholarly journals. He belongs to a school of historians who have concentrated upon analyzing the revolution as a mass movement—in Cobb's case, by studying the armies of revolutionary militia, revolutionary mass psychology, and related topics. Professor Cobb is an outspoken opponent of the "occidental" or "Atlantic" approach to eighteenth-century revolutions.

LIKE Babeuf and Buonarrotti, the English Jacobins have been somewhat victimized by a growing legend cultivated by British historians of the nineteenth and early twentieth centuries who have sought a doctrinal justification in their national past. We are handicapped, therefore, by a false perspective which has greatly exaggerated the historical importance and genuine influence of a small group. Despite their wealth, cultivation, and a liberalism coupled with the best of intentions, . . . the English Jacobins were essentially foreigners in their own country, isolated from the masses who loathed them as hard-driving bosses, and ineffective as a political pressure group. The movement of the Jacobins *per se,* or more exactly that of the Dissenters (Presbyterians, Independents, Baptists), is no doubt interesting on several counts: as a minority isolated by discriminatory measures which it did not succeed in having repealed; as set apart by superior education which . . . was the best obtainable during the period; . . . finally, as a group identifiable in terms of family ties and economic interest (hence the expression "Dissenting Interest"). The Sect, as it was called, was not a genuine political party but a great clan animated chiefly by moral and religious sentiments. It was a clan which led a life apart, that always had at least a foothold in the United States. Why did this group, despite its cultural contribution, have so little influence once the Great Revolution had broken out in France?

It is no doubt necessary to reword this question by focusing, not on the study of the Sect and its internal divisions (com-

From R. C. Cobb, "Les Jacobins anglais et la Révolution française," *Bulletin de la Société d' histoire moderne,* série 12, nº 14, vol. 59 (1960), pp. 2–5. Reprinted by permission of the Comité de la Société d'histoire moderne. Translated by the Editor.

mon to all Protestant movements), but on the broader horizon of the whole nation. The Jacobins enjoyed little success, mostly because, for a variety of reasons, the English people at the time of the declaration of war were not in a revolutionary mood and were, rightly or wrongly, quite satisfied with the institutions which excluded them almost completely from politics. In fact, the people thought of themselves as the happiest in the world: there were none more chauvinistic in all Europe. In this instance, Mr. Palmer notwithstanding, we are dealing with a specifically English situation. The repeated political crises over the Wilkes affair were not quasi-revolutions, nor were the Gordon Riots of 1780, which were provoked by anti-Catholicism and xenophobia. . . . If there was no quasi-revolutionary situation in England during the period 1760–1805 the reason must be sought in the relative well-being of the masses . . . and in the enormous success of Methodism, an enthusiastic and emotional religion which channeled popular violence. The impact of this religion that made hard work and sobriety manifest signs of grace was eminently conservative. At no time [for instance] did the Methodists endorse the campaign for repeal [of the discriminatory legislation against Dissenters]. The religion of Wesley was indeed the bastard child of that other hippopotamus, the Anglican Church.

Though this is a heatedly controversial area, apparently living standards did advance in the cities, at least . . . in the last third of the [eighteenth] century. Only from 1810 did conditions really begin to deteriorate. [Until then] progress, in London and the great cities of the northwest, marked by increased use of meat and of common everyday articles, was notable. Thanks to the development of an industry which, by mass production methods, reached the middle and even the poor consumer, the people were better and more cheaply dressed than in 1770. The urban artisan's market was not only the luxury trade, [but particularly] in the northwest the genuine industrial prosperity depended on the large-scale patronage of the middle class. In London the people ate bread, potatoes, and meat: the John Bull of the Sign of the Royal George was no mythical personage, nor did Hogarth lie. In 1790 and 1792 the spinnery workers of Manchester were to be in the vanguard of anti-Jacobin rioting; in Birmingham it was the populace which set Priestley's house on fire. There were no food crises in England, and since 1745 political peace had rarely been breached. At the same time, for reasons which are still open to controversy, the population increased considerably. Was the cause of this increase to be found in the progress of hygiene, in more sensible clothing, in greater personal cleanliness, in better housing, in the advance of medical science, in new hospitals, in declining alcoholism, safer childbirths in the hospitals? Perhaps all of these contributed, although in the new hospitals one was likely to catch all those illnesses that one did not have before entering; smallpox was always on the rampage. But after all, there was progress which could be seen and felt, and people were not discontented with their lot.

Besides, the war against France was popular: it was an easy war which did not yet burden the majority of the people. To be sure, the press gang and its methods were detested, yet even the pressed men mutinied only rarely. Jack Tar was modest in his demands: the worst-fed sailors in all Europe fought like lions. In one sense it was the war that checked the threat of revolution. John Bull hated the French as he despised the Irish and Scotch. As the revolutionary crisis deepened, this popular patriotism became even more marked and constituted the best rampart of Church and King, of established power. The people, moreover, barely distinguished between a revolutionary France and the French of the Bourbons, both of them militaristic and menacing with their vast armies and population. In the beginning, no doubt the Corresponding Societies did enjoy a very substantial membership, particularly among skilled workers such as foremen, compositors, master shoemakers, watchmakers, etc. Yet by 1793 governmental propaganda succeeded by fighting the reformers with their own methods. (Beer was on the side of the government with the tavern keeper being a most effective anti-Jacobin propagandist.) This offensive also relied upon increasingly efficient weapons, such as Stamp Acts, Combination Laws, etc. Above all, the government feared the development of a union movement, the growth of which it succeeded in delaying.

This popular chauvinism was no doubt the main reason why the reformist movement was unsuccessful. Whoever said "Dissenter" said "Leveller," "Commonwealthman," and ultimately "Jacobin": such were the names which their enemies called them, and "Jacobin" was synonymous with Frenchman. The revolutionary cause was lost because the revolution was French. Had it been Polish or Turkish, the pro-revolutionary groups in England would have had greater chances of being heard. As things stood, the Jacobins appeared as semi-traitors, as foreigners in their own country, a prejudice which even had a certain foundation, since the leaders of the Sect owned property in the United States (and sometimes also in France), emigrating when conditions [in England] deteriorated. By 1793 all their major political figures had departed, with some of them successfully establishing themselves in France. This was hardly the most effective method of converting England! The Dissenters—men of wealth, hard drivers, austere puritans, little English Robespierres—did everything to fan the hatred felt for them by their employees. The Dissenters had condemned the poor laws as favoring the cardinal sin of laziness, just as they had condemned the great state monopolies from which they were excluded. Their complete economic liberalism alienated them from the masses as much as did their infatuation for a revolution the meaning of which they failed to grasp.

We are indeed dealing here with fearful misunderstandings. As far as the Dissenters were concerned, the revolution was the work of God, opening the Reign of the Just! . . . According to this logic poor Pitt became the anti-Christ. On the French side there were similar misunderstandings: the French clubs entertained delusions about the strength of the revolutionary movement in England, having relied on the publications of the Corresponding Societies and on the somewhat sanguine hallucinations of a few English emissaries who had made the pilgrimage to Paris. Just as the English people light-heartedly accepted the war against revolutionary France because they were sure of an easy and painless victory, the French of the Year II were convinced that their English "brothers" were only awaiting a signal to depose *Georges Dandin* [King George III] and his minister. French and English Jacobins were caught in mutual mystification.

Thus the basic fact was simply the absence of a revolutionary spirit in England. Verbal pointillism over the word "democracy" is useless as it proves nothing at all. Granted that there was a strong movement in favor of parliamentary reform which, however, was arrested by a war which ushered in the two most reactionary decades of modern English history. Thanks to anti-French chauvinism, even the poor mad king regained a little of his popularity. The Church recovered a sort of virginity as a peculiarly national institution allied to John Bull, good beer, and the visceral anti-Jacobinism of the masses.

Though Jacobins were no more than voices crying in the wilderness, their failure was not complete. In the century following, the aims of the great dissenting academies of Warrington and Hackney were to be more fully and durably realized in the University of London, open to all without religious discrimination; the Jacobins themselves found worthy disciples in the Philosophical Radicals, who were more in touch with English realities.

The Spread of French Revolutionary Ideas in Ireland

H. L. CALKIN

Homer L. Calkin, the author of this article, is an American historian formerly with American University and the National Archives, and presently with the United States Department of State. He has published several articles on the French and American revolutions and on Ireland during the eighteenth century in professional journals in Paris, Dublin, and the United States.

POLITICAL and philosophic ideas are frequently not confined to a single geographic area. Ideas originating in one nation reach individuals and groups in other countries where they may be largely accepted. This is often true where two countries undergo a period of crisis and the ideas developed in one may be adopted in the other country where political and economic conditions further such acceptance.

During the last quarter of the eighteenth century, Ireland was influenced, not only by certain groups in North America, but also by European countries that had undergone revolutionary changes. The American colonies' efforts to gain their independence in turn stimulated greater Irish efforts to conquer a larger measure of freedom. France, which during the period of the French Revolution had carried the principles of liberty and equality further than had North America, served as Ireland's model in her quest for fuller political expression of her national identity.

In the past the American and French Revolutions have received much attention since these two peoples had pioneered in casting off ancient institutions and restrictions. In this context, however, Ireland's role should not be forgotten. Our aim here is to show not merely the extent to which the French revolutionary ideas had penetrated Ireland, but also to trace the initial steps of the Irish Revolution.

For a long time Ireland and France had enjoyed fairly close connections, as the Catholic religion served to tie the two countries together. Earlier, Louis XIV and James II had been good friends, while Irish priests continued to receive their education in French schools. Both countries had frequently faced England as the common enemy. Circumstances such as these had made for an occasionally very close relation between the two.

From its beginnings, the French Revolution was enthusiastically received in Ireland. According to one contemporary it was "but the spark which set the combustible

From H. L. Calkin, "La Propagation en Irlande des Idées de la Révolution française," *Annales historiques de la Révolution française,* XXXII (1955), 143–160. Reprinted by permission of *Annales historiques de la Révolution française*. Translated by the Editor.

matter on fire; but the gunpowder was there before the French revolution was in contemplation." Many Irishmen were convinced that the French were gaining rights such as political and religious freedom, parliamentary, political and social reform, liberation of people and land from oppressive controls, long sought in Ireland. "Were these not the secular claims of Ireland?" inquired another contemporary. While in France land was being liberated, in Ireland the very people whose ancestors had owned the land were now barred from it. Trade, freed in France, faced "insurmountable bounds" in Ireland. Already in 1789, according to one French historian, Irish newspapers, pamphlets and public discussions generally drew upon "our ideas, our debates and our victories."

Edward Wakefield thought that "in no country in the world, perhaps, was this new French system so likely to find continuance as in Ireland." The Irish "sympathized most sincerely with the French people, and watched their progress to freedom with the utmost anxiety." In the French victories they saw "the promise of a new freedom for all oppressed peoples." From its onset, the French Revolution was generally regarded as welcome in Ireland, and as Romilly wrote at the end of two years, "the French Revolution there has always been universally popular; and if the enthusiasm which it has kindled should anywhere break out in acts of violence, it will certainly be first in Ireland." The French were aware of such sentiments and hoped to exploit them. In 1792 [for example] French agitators sought to provoke a revolution in Ireland: "It is there that the infamous banditti in France expect the explosion will happen." In this way England, France's stubborn foe, might be dealt a death-blow.

For a long time Irishmen had advocated political and economic liberty. The American and French Revolutions intensified the desire to obtain such national freedom and individual rights. Public orators, journalists, pamphleteers and others responded by invoking French revolutionary ideas such as republicanism, liberty, equality, Jacobinism, land reform, etc.—political and philosophic ideas which they adapted to the political, economic, social and religious conditions prevailing in Ireland and spread among different sections of the people.

In and of themselves new ideas and an excellent propaganda machine are not enough if the means of dissemination are lacking. Even without the benefit of modern instruments such as radio, films and television, Ireland was not bereft of means of communication: newspapers, posters, proclamations, celebrations commemorating events in France, visits by Frenchmen were among the ways in which many Irishmen were won over. Thus the propagandists for revolutionary doctrines began by influencing the lower layers of the population among whom, quite early, many incendiary ideas circulated. Moreover, manufacturers encouraged the diffusion of the new ideas among their workers. To check this, the Irish parliament passed laws abridging freedom of the press, yet with little success since the heavier the shackles imposed the more "literature of revolutionary and even of infidel opinion was eagerly read." . . .

. . . especially by means of newspapers, the ideas and principles of men such as Roland, Robespierre and other Frenchmen were supplemented by the ideas of Irishmen which were spread throughout Ireland. Many events, ideas, organizations and practices of the French Revolution gained acceptance in Ireland where they served propaganda purposes. The enthusiasm aroused among Irishmen by the French Revolution is evinced by the many celebrations which took place, particularly at Belfast. In 1791, the July 14 anniversary of the fall of the Bastille was commemorated at Dublin and Belfast, while by 1792 many cities took part in such celebrations. . . .

Irishmen did more than drink toasts, march in parades and cheer for liberty. Collections for the French were taken ı·

at Armagh, as was done later by the United Irishmen in Belfast where, on May 18, 1792, the Society decided to send financial assistance to the French. Other revolutionary societies of northern Ireland followed suit. In the single town of Coleraine, County Londonderry, £600 were subscribed. In July 1792, a M. François read a letter written by friends of the French Constitution in Ireland before the French National Convention which offered £800 to defray state expenditures.

In order to pursue such propaganda efforts successfully, it was essential that France and Ireland keep in touch with events in each other's country. From the onset of the French Revolution "a correspondence was opened between the United Irishmen and the French revolutionary government." Under one pretext or another, representatives of the two countries traveled back and forth. For example, the Reverend William Jackson was to leave for Paris to "confer with the government." His task was "to establish a concert between the rulers of France and the malcontents of Ireland.". . .

Some Frenchmen also came to visit Ireland during this period. In 1791 and 1792, Rabaud de St. Etienne spent some time in Belfast and Dublin. "There is not a doubt but that the active interference of some French democrats among the disaffected part of the Irish Nation, their extravagant admiration of the French Revolution, and their correspondence with some of the clubs in France, contributed materially to diffuse the intoxicating poison of republicanism."

The ideas of the French Revolution were modified by these propagandists in order to adapt them directly to Irish conditions and to profit as fully as possible from already prevailing currents of public opinion. While therefore this activity affected all segments of Irish society, it did so in varying degrees. Among some sections of the population, the ideas led to immediate action, while among others they were embraced for a time but later abandoned. The majority of the people were, however, affected. Viewed in the long run, many of the events of succeeding years, as well as the Irish outlook which they mirrored, may be explained in part by this positive or negative response to the French Revolution in the United Kingdom in general and in Ireland in particular.

During a year or two [after 1789] scarcely any elements of the population viewed the consequences of the French Revolution with apprehension. Wolfe Tone said that as the Revolution progressed, Catholics "were rapidly advancing in political spirit and information." Nonetheless, the confiscation of church property and the abridgement of clerical privileges in France disturbed Irish Catholics, especially their leaders, as did the Paris massacres of 1792 which left a strong imprint. Moderate republicans came to fear a liberty which might bring such horrors in its train. According to Richard Madden, "The Catholic aristocracy, always a timid and selfish body, offered to support government in withholding their privileges; the Catholic clergy separated in a body from the Reformers, and denounced the atheism of France from their altars." In their hatred of French infidelity and atheistic republicanism, they "had become zealous royalists.". . .

Among the lower classes hatred of the English did not diminish during the revolutionary epoch. Catholic laymen and even a few priests were found in rebel ranks during the 1798 uprising, though to what extent this was the outcome of revolutionary ideas is difficult to determine. The Revolution probably not only failed to dampen, but actually intensified Catholic desire for freedom.

The case of the Catholic hierarchy was different. The confiscation of land, as well as the French Catholic dignitaries' loss of prestige, position and wealth was viewed with apprehension in Ireland, where, moreover, the Pope's denunciation of the events in France could but weaken the sympathy of priests and bishops for a revolution which was so close by. All this may explain their support of the Act of 1800, which combined the Irish and British parliaments into a single body, even though Catholic emancipation, promised in exchange for their support, failed to materialize. The clergy had nevertheless preferred negotiation to revolution. Among landlords and high officials anti-French hostility was violent. . . .

Nonetheless a negative attitude toward the French Revolution did not become generalized. The passion for liberty and the republic was strongest among the Presbyterian dissenters of Ulster, whose center was Belfast. Already in 1791 "a republican madness" had swept the North, where these dissenters were the first to take a "most decided and unqualified" stand in favor of the French Revolution. Hence it was there that the United Irishmen began advocating republicanism and separation from England. Nor did this group falter and return to old ways of thinking.

Since Presbyterians and United Irishmen together constituted the bulwark of the Irish Revolution, it seems important to speak more fully of their propaganda. At the beginning of 1792, the *Northern Star* furnished some definitions in an article dealing with the "Rights of Men and Citizens," proclaiming that:

> All men have equal Rights.
>
> These Rights are, Liberty, Security, Property, and Resistance to Oppression.
>
> Liberty is the right of saying, writing, and doing whatever we please, without injuring the State, our neighbour, or ourselves.
>
> Security is the right of being protected by the Public Force against evil doers.
>
> Property consists in every one doing what he please with his own, excepting those who are under age, or deprived of their reason.
>
> Resistance to oppression is the right of taking up arms against open violence, and illegal or tyrannical compulsion. . . .

The *Union Star,* more direct in its call to insurrection, sought to rouse men to indignation "against the impious wretch who profanely assumes the title of reigning by the Grace of God, and impudently tells the world he can do no wrong." An appeal was made to the ruling class who had handed out privileges "to murderers in order to depopulate" Ireland. They had confiscated the private possessions of the Irish and the soil of Ireland, exposing the "children to poverty and all its consequent calamities." The *Star* continued:

> Ere the grave . . . embosoms thee, make an atonement, for the vices of their predecessors; resist not the claims of a people reduced to every misery: in thy name give back the properties that thy nation wrested from a suffering people, and let the descendants of those English ruffians restore to Irishmen their country, and to their country liberty. 'Tis rather late to trifle—one fortunate breeze may do it, and then woe be to him who was a tyrant, or who is unjust. . . .

In time, the call to insurrection became even more pressing. A manifesto urged the Irish to "arise like a great and powerful people, determined to live free or die." They were to arm and to throw themselves "like lions" upon their enemies. The appeal continued thus:

> War alone must occupy every mind and every hand in Ireland until its long-oppressed soil be purged of all its enemies. Vengeance, Irishmen, vengeance on your oppressors! remember that thousands of your dearest friends have perished by their merciless orders. Remember their burnings, their rackings, their torturings, their military massacres, and their legal murders. . . .

If the effectiveness of any propaganda is to be judged by the positive or negative reactions of the people, Irish insurrectionary propaganda did have some results. Insurrectionary acts did take place in several counties in 1797 and 1798, while in many regions protests on the part of discontented elements were widespread. It was at this time that the French, under the command of General Humbert, landed at Killala on August 22, 1798, kindling Irish hopes by proclaiming that they had "come to support your courage, to share your dangers, to join their arms, and to mix their blood with yours in the sacred cause of liberty. . . . Union! liberty! the Irish Republic! such is our shout, let us march—our hearts are devoted to you; our glory is in your happiness."

Indeed the French and Irish penetrated half way to Dublin before the governmental forces were able to stave off the threat. Nonetheless, the danger had loomed so large that it was one of the factors which led the English to advocate the Act of Union of 1800 which placed both countries under one parliament.

Even after the elimination of the danger of rebellion in 1798, the United Irishmen remained active. An Irish catechism was published and circulated "for the purpose of keeping the flame of it alive." It is of interest to consider the objectives of this organization during the several years which followed their initial contact with the French Revolution and after they had organized an uprising seeking secession from England. The preamble, which is worth quoting in its entirety, clearly states the position of the United Irishmen. One might well have called this the "rights of men" or the "rights of an Irishman":

> I believe in the Irish Union, in the supreme majesty of the people, in the equality of men, in the lawfulness of insurrection, and of resistance to oppression. I believe in the revolution founded on the rights of man in the natural and imprescriptible right of all the Irish citizens to the land. I believe the soil, or any part of it, cannot be transferred without the consent of the people, or their representatives, convened and authorised by the votes of every man having arrived at the age of twenty-one years. I believe the land, or any of it, cannot become the property of any man, but by purchase, or as rewards for forwarding and preserving the publick liberty. I believe our present connexion with England must be speedily dissolved. I believe that old age, pregnant women, and labour should be honoured. I believe that treason is the crime of betraying the people. I believe religious distinctions are only protected by tyrants. I believe applying the lands of the church to relieve old age, to give education and protection to infancy, will be more acceptable to a united people, than maintaining lazy hypocrites and ravenous tythegatherers. In this faith I mean to live, or bravely die. . . .

Throughout the French Revolution, many British and Irish political leaders had tried to draw attention to the threat posed to Ireland by a movement such as the one in France. The Revolution had barely begun when T. Somers Cocks was writing to Miles: "I dare say the spirit of liberty which has broken out in France will extend itself to other countries." Miles, in the meantime, was writing from Paris to his Irish friend, Count Newenham: "Believe me, nothing has been done as yet in this country worthy of being imitated in yours." Shortly after, he wrote once again: "Wait the conclusion of the Revolution in France before you think of introducing any of its regulations into Ireland, and even then, examine them well, and see that they are adapted to your habits, your maxims of government, and your prejudices."

Such warnings proved useless and, as we have seen, the passion for liberty continued to grow among the Presbyterians of Belfast. . . .

The Act of Union of 1800 ended for a good many years any possibility that the Irish people might gain either independence or extensive individual liberties. Of the three revolutions—the American, the French and the Irish—the last had enjoyed the least success. Its ideas and principles, almost identical to those of the French, testified to the same concern for liberty and individual equality. Like the French, the Irish revolutionaries would have toppled their ruling class, pursued a liberal and even anti-clerical policy, confiscated the property of the absentee landlords to turn the land over to the Irish masses.

These aims could not be realized in the eighteenth century. Against a counter-revolution fomented by British opposition and supported by armed force, the Irish, inferior in numbers, lacked sufficient cohesion to act effectively. Nonetheless, Irish adherence to French ideas led England to look upon this adjoining part of the kingdom with apprehension and disapproval. Among the chief Irish objectives was parliamentary reform, a measure which England was bound to oppose as applied to Ireland, since such reform was scarcely tolerated in England itself. To carry out legislative reforms and Catholic emancipation might have precipitated uprisings and agitation in England at the very time that the country was involved in an important continental war. Under these circumstances there was no question of tolerating political turmoil in one part of the empire. Had Ireland enjoyed the freedom to proceed with the realization of its political ideas, a complete break between the two countries would have taken place. The union of the two parliaments, imposed by England, put off such changes, at least for the time being.

What could not be accomplished during the eighteenth century had to be postponed until the nineteenth and twentieth centuries. Instead of undergoing a revolution bringing about radical changes within a short time, Ireland was obliged to follow a much slower evolutionary course to obtain the desired reforms. While the final result may have been the same, the process intensified Irish hostility toward England. One may thus conclude that the French Revolution's influence, however great, failed to produce the result that might have been expected; for Ireland, because of its proximity to Great Britain, was unable to throw off the yoke which it had worn for centuries.

From Joseph II to the Jacobin Trials

ERNST WANGERMANN

Ernst Wangermann, the author of *From Joseph II to the Jacobin Trials* from which the following selection is taken, is a British historian of Austrian descent who has recently been appointed Lecturer in Modern History at the University of Leeds. Aside from his book, based on an Oxford University Ph.D. thesis, Mr. Wangermann has contributed articles on Austrian and German history to *Collier's Encyclopedia* and the *New Cambridge Modern History*.

The "Jacobin Trials" of 1794 in Austria and Hungary saw the condemnation for high treason of a number of professional men and army officers sympathetic to liberalism and the French Revolution. Many of the accused had been ardent supporters of the enlightened policies of Joseph II and of his successor, Leopold II. The trial of these middle-class liberals thus indicated that the new monarch, Francis II, intended to depart from the liberalism of his predecessors.

IF one is to pass a fair judgement on the apprehensions of Count Pergen and the subsequent activities of his ministry, it is necessary to investigate the actual strength and character of the active internal opposition in the Habsburg dominions in the troubled months of 1793–4. The evidence is inadequate, but must serve as far as it goes.

Out of the frustrated political aspirations of the non-privileged had developed an active political opposition to the policies of Francis II's government. But the government, so far from yielding to this opposition continued and consolidated its policies, and revived the Ministry of Police for the purpose of dealing with the opposition. This left opponents of the government's policies with the alternative of either discontinuing their opposition and keeping their views to themselves, or of getting together unobtrusively with like-minded men to organize and co-ordinate their opposition with the aim of securing a change in policy while such a change was still feasible.

According to all the evidence available, the various activities which have gone into history as the Jacobin Conspiracy were little more than such an attempt to organize and co-ordinate the active opposition to the policies of Francis II's government.

There already existed a strong tradition of regular gatherings of men of "advanced" opinions in places where foreign newspapers and periodicals were available, a tradition which dated from the days of Joseph II. As the political vanguard of the non-privileged turned into the political opposition under Francis II, these gatherings graduated into "democratic" or "Jacobin" assemblies in the official parlance of the time. For the increasing official disfavour in which they and their ideas were held

From Ernst Wangermann, *From Joseph II to the Jacobin Trials* (Oxford, 1959), pp. 133–169. Reprinted by permission of the Clarendon Press.

by the government could only strengthen the democrats' desire to meet like-minded people, to discuss political developments with them, and to exchange ideas.

With the gradual disappearance of foreign newspapers and periodicals at the instance of Counts Sauer, Pergen, and Saurau, and even more with the imposition of an uncomfortable and obnoxious police supervision over all coffee-houses and inns, the scene of political discussions shifted from public to private places beyond the reach of the watchful eye of the police. And within the four walls of private establishments the general tone of the discussions became more radical, hopes more exalted, and projects more daring.

Such democratic gatherings existed probably in all provinces of the monarchy, but the evidence we have is necessarily of those whose activities eventually brought down upon themselves the full force of the police, i.e., those in Innsbruck, Upper Styria, Vienna, and Hungary.

The Innsbruck circle consisted entirely of university students who were brought together by an Italian enthusiast for the French Revolution. The latter, a servant of Sir Levett Hanson, instructed his young hearers in the history of the Revolution, as a result of which the latter decided to dedicate themselves to the cause of liberty and equality.

The Styrian circles, of course, consisted in the main of the burghers' deputies to the diet and some of their electors, who had been compelled to give up their promising campaign for peasant representation in the diet, but who were still trying to achieve full equality with the upper orders in the organization of the Styrian Estates.

In Vienna there was more than one group, though the different groups overlapped to a certain extent. The most important was that which gathered in the house of Baron Andreas Riedel, the confidant of Leopold II, who had tried to induce his successor to desist from the war against France. Here Lieutenant Hebenstreit was a frequent and honoured attender, and expounded his view that human misery would continue so long as men said "mine" and "thine" and refused to have things in common. In this circle high and low seemed to mix on equal terms.

A more purely intellectual group was that of Professor Wollstein, the Director of the Vienna School of Veterinary Surgery. This circle included the poet and magistrate Prandstätter, ex-Professor Neupauer, and the lawyer Dr. Jutz.

Lastly, there was the circle of the poet Blumauer and his landlord Johann Hackl, which included such diverse personalities as Martinovics, the Abbé Strattmann, a friend of Gottfried van Swieten, and the police commissioner of Lemberg, Troll, who had carried out some secret assignments for Leopold under Gotthardi's direction.

The members of each of these groups were mostly acquainted also with those of the others. Apart from the houses of Riedel, Wollstein, and Hackl, the premises of a small number of "democratic" shops in the centre of Vienna were used by them for short gatherings and discussions during the day.

The chief occupation of all these groups was political discussion, especially of developments in France, and the circulation of prohibited newspapers and books amongst themselves. Clauer's *Kreuzzug wider die Franken* was avidly read by Dirnböck and the Styrian burghers' deputies. Tom Paine's *Rights of Man* circulated in a French translation. Prohibited newspapers were smuggled in from Salzburg. News of French victories was always received with general acclamation, as it seemed to bring nearer prospects of peace.

The social life of the groups was fairly well developed, and there were numerous dinner parties, especially when there were guests from abroad or from other provinces to be entertained. When spirits were high, the *Marseillaise* and *Ça ira* would be sung.

The political activity of the democrats consisted above all in their sustained effort to spread their own ideas among their fellow citizens. This was done either by the direct method of introducing new members into the groups, or by disseminating leaflets, pamphlets, songs, and so forth, both of popular and more refined appeal. Riedel was the author of several satirical pamphlets. Prandstätter translated Batthyány's *Ad Amicam Aurem,* and Gilovsky one of Robespierre's celebrated speeches. Both Martinovics and Riedel worked on a "Catechism," setting out their ideas in that form of question and answer which Jesuit education had made so familiar. Georg Ruszitska, a member of the Riedel group, showed his prowess by composing an appeal to the peasants to resist the reimposition of labour services, which Jelline, a very ardent democrat, undertook to translate into Czech. Hebenstreit was the author of a long Latin poem entitled *Homo Hominibus,* in which the usual ideas of the Enlightenment were interspersed with utopian socialist notions of common ownership.

Hebenstreit, who was nothing if not versatile, was also the creator of the most successful of the "Jacobin" propaganda efforts, the *Eipeldauerlied.* To words written by Captain Beck, who had died in 1793, he had supplied the melody which helped to carry the words far and wide. The *Eipeldauerlied* strikes a new revolutionary note, since it assumes that Francis has given himself up completely to the aristocracy, and for the first time completely identifies Emperor and aristocracy:

> Take a good look at our emperor boy
> Who's sticking to the nobles.
> King Louis with aristocracy did toy;
> That's why he came unstuck.[1]

Some of these pamphlets were still unfinished at the time of the arrests. Most of them circulated only in handwritten copies. Riedel, however, insisted that Hebenstreit's *Homo Hominibus* ought to be printed, and the manuscript was finally taken to a printer in Steinamanger who was a relation of one of the members of Riedel's group. But it was already too late. Before the corrected proofs could be returned to the printers, Hebenstreit and his friends were under lock and key.

The chief limitation of the democratic propaganda in Vienna was its almost complete lack of contact with the peasants of the surrounding countryside. In this respect the Styrian democrats enjoyed an important advantage. From the days of the joint campaign of burghers and peasants for constitutional reform in Styria, there existed a close contact between the opposition in town and country. Hence democratic propaganda in Styria was also organized around the commutation of tithes. The peasants looked to the burghers' deputies to draw up their petitions for them. And Franz Haas and Joseph Wenninger were not the men to miss such an opportunity of disseminating their political ideas and attacking their opponents.

An important part of the democratic propaganda both in Styria and Vienna was propaganda for peace. Among the varied political opinions confessed to in the course of the subsequent trials, opposition to the war against France was common to all who were investigated. To strengthen the opposition against the war, good use could be made of any news of French military successes. The ostentatious clerical support that was given to the war was an easy target for democratic satire. The passage of French prisoners of war presented opportunities for most effective demonstrations of the desire for peace and friendship with the people of France. And the Styrian experience in the technique of political campaigning provided an excellent foundation for an organized peace campaign with circulars, petitions, and signatures, which was initiated by the burgher deputies of the Judenburg district.

The problem of giving some sort of organization to the democratic groups and winning new members for them on a large

[1] Schauts enker Kaiser Kind nur an,
Mit'n Adel tut er's halten,
Der Ludwig hat's halt a so than,
D'rum haben s'n ja nit g'halten.

scale, so that they might become instruments for effective action other than propaganda, was only just beginning to be tackled at the time of the arrests.

Baron Riedel introduced the idea of using a sign by which all those in agreement with the aims of the groups could recognize each other and thus form some idea as to the numerical strength of the democrats. Some of the more ardent younger members, among them the physician Dr. Menz, devised a formula for an oath to be taken, "in the name of Nature, Reason and Freedom," and pledging unceasing struggle against despots and fanaticism. When early in July 1794 a deputation from Styrian burghers which included Dirnböck came to Vienna, they sought and found contact with some of the Vienna democrats. As a result long discussions on the French Constitution took place. A strong common attachment to political freedom kindled the desire for a closer union between them. To cement such a closer union the Styrian deputies joined their Viennese friends in a quasi-masonic ceremony on top of a hill in the Brühl near Vienna at which the above oath was taken.

The news of this procedure seems to have been received with satisfaction in the democratic circles, but there is no evidence that it was repeated by anyone else.

In Hungary the democratic groups were more numerous than anywhere else in the Habsburg dominions. A very large group existed in the capital and met in the house of Ferenc Abaffy, a prominent aristocratic reformer in the Diet of 1790. Among the members of this group we find József Hajnóczy, author of several learned books refuting aristocratic and clerical pretensions, the ardent young Ferenc Szentmarjay who translated Rousseau's *Contrat Social* into Hungarian, Professor Antal Kreil of the University of Pest, and many other intellectuals, lawyers and civil servants. Democratic groups, some large, some small, met regularly in the provincial centres of Kaschau, Grosswardein, and Güns.

The propaganda activities of the Hungarian groups differed little from those of the Austrian ones. Martinovics, however, who abandoned all hope of frightening Francis II into a change of policy, assumed the leadership of the Hungarian democrats in the spring of 1794. Claiming to be in contact with the Committee of Public Safety, and holding out the prospect of French aid, he persuaded them to set up a regular underground organization called *Gesellschaft der Freiheit und Gleichheit.* Its "Catechism" envisaged a Hungarian republic freed from feudal dominion. To acquire the necessary strength for the initial rebellion, Martinovics founded a second secret society—the *Gesellschaft der Reformierten*—which had the specific purpose of attracting the nationalist gentry to the cause of rebellion, so that they might provide its spearhead as they had done in 1789 and 1790. Naturally, the gentry were kept ignorant of the anti-feudal *Gesellschaft der Freiheit und Gleichheit,* which was waiting in the wings to reap the harvest of the victorious rebellion by transforming it into a middle-class revolution. By the summer of 1794, Martinovics and his "directors"—Hajnóczy, Laczkovics and Szentmarjay for the democrats and Count Jakab Sigray for the gentry—had recruited about 300 members to their respective secret societies.

No one among the Austrian "Jacobins" shared the Hungarians' clear political perspective. There was little awareness that the realization of their aims might require revolutionary action. Consequently the possibility and nature of such action remained the subject of purely theoretical speculation on which the most varied views were being expressed. Riedel himself seems to have regarded the "dullness" of the Austrian peasantry as an obstacle which would prevent revolutionary action for a long time to come. The socialist Hebenstreit, on the other hand, could not believe that the French and Polish peasant was more "enlightened" than the Austrian, and was convinced that the dire poverty of the artisans in the growing towns would ensure the success of a revolutionary appeal to them at any time. Neither attempted to draw any practical conclusions from their theory.

It is clear that there was no regular contact with any democratic organizations abroad. But the Riedel circle had a secret which they very much wanted to impart to the French government. Hebenstreit had been stimulated by the agrarian revolts of 1790–2 to consider the problems facing an ill-equipped peasant army in defending itself against a well-equipped cavalry. As a result, he had designed a "war-machine," based on the principle of the *chevaux de frise,* which he and his friends were convinced would be of great service to the French in their struggle against the Austrian forces and therefore help to bring the war to an end. One member of the Riedel circle, the Protestant pastor Karl Traugott Held, had a contact which finally enabled him to take the secret to the French capital.

Held came from Saxony, and was acquainted with the Polish patriot Count Soltyk, who was in Vienna in the early months of 1794 trying to buy arms for Kosciusko. Held imparted his secret to Soltyk on condition that the latter co-operated in making it available also to the French. Soltyk immediately sent a courier with the design of Hebenstreit's invention to Kosciusko, and gave Held 200 florins for the journey to Paris, as well as a letter addressed to Barsch, the Polish chargé d'affaires in Paris.

Held, accompanied by a young German, Denkmann, arrived in Basle on 28 April 1794, where the secretary of the French Embassy referred them to General Schérer. The latter thought that the design might be of great importance, and enabled them to proceed to Paris. They arrived on 9 May, but were promptly arrested before they had a chance to acquaint the Committee of Public Safety with the purpose of their journey. However, they explained Hebenstreit's invention in writing and managed to convey the material to the committee. As a result of this and a persuasive petition, the committee decided to release them on 9 August. Whether the committee tried to make any use of the invention it is not at the moment possible to say.

Clearly, the evidence concerning the various "Jacobin" groups in the Habsburg dominions does not trace even the outlines of a powerful "conspiracy" menacing the foundations of the monarchy. The question therefore arises, why the Ministry of Police should have come to the conclusion that they did represent an acute danger, and should have so strongly insisted on ruthless counter-measures. To find a convincing answer to this question it is necessary to turn from the activities of the "Jacobin" groups to the general political situation in which these activities were carried on.

The failure of the campaign of 1793 had shattered whatever hopes of a short war had survived the earlier disasters. The preparation of the 1794 campaign involved new financial burdens (though the name of "war-tax" was avoided) and a new drain of the badly needed manpower from the land to re-form depleted regiments. The continued requirements of army provisions helped to push up prices from the already high level prevailing since the Turkish War and jeopardized supplies for the capital. The attempt to suppress exports to Revolutionary France and, after April 1794, also to Revolutionary Poland inflicted considerable dislocation on Austrian commerce and industries. Everywhere an acute lack of money and men made itself felt. To crown all, the 1794 harvest in Hungary, the monarchy's principal granary, was threatened by a severe drought.

Inevitably, the brunt of all the hardships was borne by the non-privileged, who were still waiting for the concessions which had seemed at hand at the close of Leopold's reign, but which had been shelved in that of his son.

Under these circumstances, the police reports on the general state of public opinion were bound to give rise to serious misgivings at the Ministry of Police. . . .

The opponents of enlightened despotism among the Emperor's advisers had long been proclaiming the close connexion between reforms and revolution, and had pointed to France as the classic illustration of their case. The trial of the Austrian "Jacobins" supplied them with evidence nearer home. Anger and disappointment at the abandonment of enlightened despotism had led some of its adherents into "subversive" paths. Enthusiasm for the levelling reforms of Joseph II had in most cases been the origin of the political radicalism of 1794. Some of the accused themselves emphasized this fact in the hope that it would serve as an excuse in the eyes of their judges. Thus we read in Jelline's defence: "The Enlightened reforms of the Emperor Joseph kindled a blazing fire in me; I devoured the Enlightened political literature with insatiable avidity, and my opinions became more and more republican."

Could there be a more unequivocal confirmation of the longstanding prophecies of Cardinal Migazzi and the anti-Enlightenment party? Clearly it was high time not only to abandon further reform (that had been secured in 1792) but to turn back the clock and undo the dangerous work of enlightened despotism.

The laborious effort of dismantling the edifice of enlightened reform makes up the internal history of the Habsburg dominions in the decade following the Jacobin trials. The "argument from the trials" was the decisive factor in bringing about the victory of the anti-Enlightenment party in nearly every field of government policy. . . .

Much in Little: The Dutch Revolution of 1795

R. R. PALMER

The present paper deals only with the Dutch, but its purpose is to illuminate the whole complex of war and revolution which then gripped the Western world.

The United Provinces, though very different from Bourbon France, were typical of the *ancien régime* in Europe. They were, indeed, very small. From the spire of Utrecht cathedral, on a clear day in 1794, Ann Radcliffe saw the whole of Holland and its six sister-provinces spread out before her, with fifty towns visible in the flatland from this one elevated point. The population, some 1,800,000, was less than that of the infant United States. The small size of the political unit was characteristic of that core of Europe which reached from the North Sea to the island of Malta. Small states or weak ones—the United Provinces, the Papal States, the German principalities, and most notably Poland—all faced the prospect, by the 1780's, of control or outright partition by those giants soon to be called "great powers," in whose rise Leopold von Ranke saw the chief political phenomenon of the eighteenth century. In fact, in 1787, a Prussian army invaded Holland and forcibly restored the evicted Prince of Orange. Prussia and Great Britain, by treaty, thereupon "guaranteed" the Orange regime, not so much against France, reduced to impotency by the approach of revolution, as against indigenous Dutch agitation. It was this restored regime, supported by Prussia and Britain, that fell to Dutch revolutionaries supported by France in 1795.

In the sense in which "medieval" was and is sometimes applied to the eighteenth century, the United Provinces were, if anything, more medieval than France, having never felt the hand of a unifying and modernizing absolute monarchy. Medieval liberties persisted as inherited rights. Each province and each town was an autonomous entity, jealous of all powers above it in the federal structure. The estates general represented the estates of the seven provinces and could not act without unanimity. Naval affairs were purposely divided among numerous boards and colleges, whose cumbersome operation was one cause of the decline of the Dutch fleet. Other executive and financial business was similarly impeded. The stadholderate had become legally hereditary in the House of Orange, but the stadholder's authority was narrowly circumscribed, and there had been long decades with no stadholder at all. As elsewhere in Europe—in Venice, the German free cities, most of the Swiss cantons, and the Belgian provinces; in the British parliamentary system and in France and the other great monarchies—the exercise of public authority had fallen into the hands of a relatively few interconnected families, the oligarchies, patriciates, and aristocracies of the Old Regime. Among the Dutch the ruling group was called the *regenten* or

From R. R. Palmer, "Much in Little: The Dutch Revolution of 1795," *Journal of Modern History,* XXVI (1954), 15–35. Reprinted by permission of The University of Chicago Press.

"regents"; others were the *ingezetene* or "inhabitants"; there was no such thing as Dutch citizenship. Thirty-six regents constituted the governing council of Amsterdam, a city of 200,000. They held office for life and chose their own successors; they controlled the Amsterdam delegation in the estates of Holland and, through Holland, influenced the estates general of the union.

The republic had been founded in the sixteenth century on the rock of Calvinism, which was the established religion. Nevertheless, about a third of the people were Roman Catholic; and Catholics, Jews, Mennonites, and other Protestant sectaries made up over 40 per cent of the population. They were all peaceably tolerated, but they occupied an inferior status. Only the Dutch Reformed church could ring church bells and carry on public worship. Only its adherents had any role in the conduct of government, military or naval command, the Bank of Amsterdam, or the East India Company.

In all such matters Hogendorp, a regent himself, saw no difference in principle between the United Provinces and Bourbon France, or between the Dutch and French revolutions, both of which, in his view, represented the conflict between established and inherited right upheld by a privileged church and the revolutionary force of "democracy," as he called it. It is worth noting, too, as an evidence of prevailing conditions, that Hogendorp, despite his conservatism, declared in 1790 that the main problem for the Dutch was in fact to admit larger segments of the population into public life.

There were, of course, important differences between the Dutch revolution and the French. The Dutch revolutionaries had no monarchy, no significant nobility, and no powerfully organized Catholic church to combat. Their revolution was without agrarian upheaval, without general confiscation, without emigration, and without terror. As a small people, lacking in power, they developed little of the French crusading impulse to liberate the world. They were described by all travelers as phlegmatic and sensible, disinclined to abstract theorizing and to exaggerated idealism. Though by no means unexcitable—an Amsterdam mob had once torn John De Witt limb from limb—the Dutch were scarcely capable of the salvationist ecstasy or monomaniac fanaticism in which Jacobinism has sometimes been thought to consist. Nor does the Dutch revolution fit a Marxist pattern, since virtually all participants were "bourgeois" in a Marxist sense. Hogendorp, the Dutch patrician, when ejected from office in 1795, neither emigrated nor took to arms nor secluded himself in his country estate, as a French nobleman might have done; he turned to private business and built up the family fortunes by strictly mercantile pursuits. The Dutch revolution was not an affair between bourgeois and feudal noble.

That despite such differences the Dutch movement resembled the agitation in other countries may help to suggest what the issues in this revolutionary era were. The following is a narrative of the Dutch revolution, since even the bare succession of events seems little known outside the Netherlands; but the narrative will be punctuated with analytical observations, to bring the story within the wider history of the time.

The Army of the North, which crossed the Waal in January 1795, was a branch of those formidable forces created in France during the Terror. Robespierre had been dead, and the Terror ended, for half a year. Since the opening of the annual campaign, in the spring of 1794, the French had been spectacularly successful. They had driven the coalition armies out of France and across Belgium, whence the Austrians and Prussians retreated into Germany, while the British and Dutch fell back in great confusion into the Netherlands. The French began to enter Dutch territory south of the Waal as early as July 1794. The Netherlands were thrown into a turmoil in which three forces may be distinguished: first, the French, or rather the expectation of the French arrival; second, the native Dutch revolutionaries; and, third, the existing Dutch government of William V, carried on through Van de Spiegel, the "pensionary" or executive officer of Holland.

The policy of the French was to use the great wealth of the Dutch to their own advantage—to bring the Dutch resources, the gold, foreign exchange, and commercial connections of the Dutch banks, and the Dutch shipping and navy around to the side of revolution in the struggle against counterrevolution, represented by French royalists and *émigrés,* the coalition powers, and, above all, Great Britain. The French preferred that the Dutch stage a revolution of their own, drive out the Orange family, and set up a revolutionary republic which should be a willing and co-operative ally. Such a regime, it was thought, would serve the common cause better and exploit Dutch resources more fully than a regime of conquest and subjugation. Dutch *émigrés,* in France, led by General Daendels and in secret communication with revolutionaries at home, worked for this same goal of an independent, but pro-French and revolutionary, Dutch republic. The French, who by this time took a national pride in their Revolution and were a little inclined to scoff at the timid and genteel revolutionism of other peoples, while threatening military conquest if matters were too long delayed, consented to wait for a native Dutch upheaval.

An absurd situation was thus created, in which the terrible French Republic, with its irresistible armies, waited for its small neighbor to have its own revolution, while the Dutch revolutionists, though willing enough, refused to commit themselves until the French army was on the spot. Who were these revolutionists?

They were no longer led by the *émigrés,* such as Daendels, the Dutch refugees from the Orange coup of 1787; they were the Dutchmen living in Holland and the other provinces, and they included a few regents, a great many burghers of substance outside the old regent families, a great many common people, who traditionally favored the House of Orange but had come to dislike the regents, a great many Catholics, who in the United Provinces (as in Ireland), being an out-group, looked with favor on the French Revolution despite the horrified outcries of Catholics in other quarters.

"Jacobin" clubs existed in all the Dutch cities. The data on their number, membership, and activities illuminate the central question in any revolution, namely, to what degree it was "willed" by the people. Dutch leaders were realistic on this matter. As Van Dam, an active figure in the Amsterdam club, wrote to the *émigré* Daendels in February 1794: "The French patriot seizes arms and flies to the place where he can use them in the cause of freedom, but the Dutch patriot, knowing that his redeemer is near the border, knits his forehead, sighs, lights his pipe, and waits for the same freedom while having a smoke in his back parlor." In their Amsterdam club, he went on, whose members were of such standing that they knew every important person in the city, they had begun to make three lists: one of persons willing to act for the "French principles," one of those who would allow such principles to enter, and one of the doubtful. He could honestly put only a hundred persons in the first list. Yet, he added, seven-eighths of the population thought itself "patriot" in the sense of being anti-Orange. At the same time, in February 1794—that is, during the French Terror—a similar analysis was given by Isaac J. A. Gogel, a man who was to play a large role in Holland during the next twenty years. The Dutch, he said, would not make a revolution but would accept one; the French should bring in, with their armies, a ready-made constitution, abolishing the privileges, guilds, provinces, corporations, monopolies, magistracies, and law courts of the old Dutch regime; they should also institute a temporary *gouvernement révolutionnaire* equipped with a revolutionary tribunal and guillotine. Indeed, as a man of the eighteenth century, lacking national feeling, Gogel rejoiced in the prospect of the incorporation of the Dutch, Belgians, and French into one great freedom-giving republic, by which "Carthage" (i.e., England) would be ruined, and "30,000,000 men, forming one people of brothers, would transmit to their posterity a sublime happiness hitherto unknown to mortals." This lyric sally, being addressed to the French civil representative with the Army of the North, may be taken less as visionary rapture than as an urgent appeal to the French army to arrive.

The number of clubs and of their members rapidly increased during 1794. In June there were thirty-four clubs in Amsterdam and twelve in Utrecht—for the Dutch clubs, like the London Corresponding Society at the same time, were organized in neighborhood units with 100 or so members in each. At Amsterdam at this time there were 5,000 or 6,000 members; at Utrecht perhaps 800; at Leiden and Haarlem 300 or 400 each. Such figures represented from 1 to 3 per cent of the population or from 4 to 12 in 100 adult males. These are the same proportions that Brinton found for the Jacobin clubs in the larger towns of France at the height of the revolution.

The clubs were known collectively as the "Leather Apron," and the bulk of the membership was composed of tradesmen. The Dutch clubs, in fact, like the London Corresponding Society, seem to have had a truly working-class membership in larger proportion than did the French Jacobins. Publicly they called themselves "reading societies." It is probable that reading and discussion actually took place, for the eighteenth-century revolution in Holland, as in France and America, saw the beginnings of a popular press, and the clubs served as places in which educated persons spread ideas to a half-literate lower class. Club members arrested by the government in October testified that they read newspapers and certain Dutch books, such as Pieter Paulus' *Menshenvriend;* one named Thomas Paine's *Rights of Man.* A conservative informant of the government declared that the purpose of the clubs was to "control the inhabitants' way of thinking on religious worship and government," to obstruct recruiting, and to "represent government to the inhabitants as hateful and unbearable."

Besides merely reading and talking, the clubs were engaged in secret activity, more or less known to the government, which, however, failed to repress it or took only enough half-measures to make itself "hateful." The clubs stored up arms and exchanged deputations with one another. The Amsterdam club was in frequent communication, legally treasonous, with the French. On the night of July 31 a great assemblage of club delegates from all the seven provinces met at Amsterdam; it authorized Van Dam and Gogel to proceed secretly to French headquarters in Belgium, to learn the terms on which the Dutch, if they opened their gates, would be spared the fate of a conquered province meted out to Belgium. The French reply, as before, was that the Dutch would be treated as allies if they staged their own revolution.

So revolutionary preparations went ahead. Committees made ready to move in and replace existing officials in the various town halls. Soldiers in the garrisons were won over. Plans were laid to assemble insurrectionary crowds. At Utrecht, a city of some fifteen thousand, two thousand persons were in the "secret" for yielding the place to the French, and the garrison of twenty-eight hundred expressed its disinclination to resist. Still the revolution did not come off. The country was full of retreating British soldiers and of Dutch units employed by, and in part loyal to, the estates general and the Prince of Orange. Revolutionary leaders felt themselves to be insecure—they wanted a safe and orderly revolution. They appealed to the French, promising to rise on the first appearance of the French army. The Amsterdam revolutionary committee wrote to the French: "Look with compassion on a party that extends its hands out to you and has no prospect but total ruin if you abandon it!" The Amsterdam club feared repression by the stadholder's government. Gogel also expressed a fear of the Left. "Nothing is easier," he wrote to the French, "than for us to raise popular disturbances, but we want no revolution unless we can guard our fellow-citizens from murder and pillage, and. . . ." He wanted the French to move in at once, to preserve order.

Meanwhile the existing Dutch government, the third recognizable party in this chaos, found itself paralyzed. That only a small minority of the population would take any revolutionary initiative is very true. More significant, however, and making the country really susceptible to revolution is the fact that, to all appearances, the minority willing to fight for the existing government was equally small. The regime of regents and stadholder was under great physical pressure; its army and its allies were routed, and the French enemy was at the border. There was a feeling of hopelessness and the dread that resistance to the French would lead to retribution. Yet it is impossible not to conclude that the regime was morally bankrupt. In the crisis it could not appeal to its own subjects; it commanded no loyalty, except among a few. . . .

So the country fell into dissolution, and its leaders and allies into mutual recrimination. The debacle was due, many Orangists held, to the failure of the British to give enough help. If only the British had given as much aid to the Dutch as they did to the Austrians! If only they had spared a few more troops and granted two or three more million pounds! According to the British, the disaster was due to the Dutch refusal to help themselves. They could not budge from the sloth of peacetime habits, reported the British minister: "In truth, our exertions in their behalf, instead of producing, as they ought, proportionable efforts on their part, appear hitherto to have had the direct contrary tendency; that is to say, that in proportion as we *add* to our share of the joint stock of ways and means, their pedlar-like spirit leads them . . . to subduct from theirs, so as to leave the sum total nearly as before."

The British army, feebly commanded by the Duke of York, behaved very badly on its retreat through the Netherlands, whereas the incoming French, under firm discipline, made a good impression. Such is the unanimous testimony of Orangist and hence Anglophile sources and of the Prussian representative at The Hague. Peasants, if armed, preferred to fight the British; the city of Delft refused to receive British wounded. One Orangist complained that French intrigues had done less than British pillaging to alienate the Dutch people. All agreed that the Duke of York was incompetent. All the old fear and dislike of the British was awakened. Even Orangists, who had owed their position since 1787 to British support, were troubled and divided. Some believed, as did the patriots, that Britain was dangerous as either friend or foe. As lately as 1784 the Dutch had suffered for taking part in the war of American independence; though Britain was the loser and the Dutch presumably on the winning side, the Dutch had been obliged to accept British penetration of the Molucca Islands.

As for the French, not only did their troops preserve discipline on entering the country, but their official demands were held to a minimum. Dutch moderates, the most numerous element, having dreaded *la guillotine, réquisition, assignats, égalité,* etc., were delighted at the reasonableness of the French officials. At first, the French stipulated only that the stadholder must go and that the Dutch must join the war against England. They thus built on the broadest possible basis of pro-French feeling. Moderates agreed with radicals; burgomasters sat down with incendiaries. Riots in Amsterdam and elsewhere unseated the authorities; revolutionary committees set up provisional governments. Meanwhile, William V retired to England. Here one of his first actions was to sanction British occupation of the Cape of Good Hope and Dutch colonies in the East and West

Indies. His own followers were thrown into consternation, and many Dutch became convinced that war against England was necessary to preserve the empire as well as to secure the revolution.

The Batavian Republic was proclaimed in January 1795, but for three years it had no constituted or settled government, even on paper. We may take the period until August 1797 as a unit. It was a period of conflict ending in frustration, resoundingly signalized by the repudiation in August 1797 of the first proposed constitution, and preparing the way for a radical-democrat phase in 1798.

The French in this period, considering that they were in military occupation, interfered relatively little in internal Dutch affairs. The French aim was still to use Holland in the war against Great Britain. This aim did not constitute forcible interference, since many Dutch were in favor of it. Nevertheless when the terms of the treaty between the French and Batavian republics became known (the treaty of The Hague of May 1795), many in the Netherlands were disappointed. The Batavian Republic was required not only to declare war on England but to maintain a French occupying army at Dutch expense, to accept French paper money, to cede Flushing and the mouth of the Scheldt, and to pay an indemnity of 100,000,000 florins. This was severe treatment for an alleged ally, but not severe enough to alienate Dutch revolutionaries from France, since they saw no alternative except capitulation to England and the House of Orange. The brute facts of war and counterrevolution made the Dutch dependent on the French republican government and republican army —as, indeed, happened to the French themselves, who were neither predominantly republican nor war-loving in these years, but who became dependent on those who "saved" them from the British and the Bourbons.

It is necessary to remember also that the French government, after the fall of Robespierre, no longer represented the most extreme leftist, or democratic, opinion to be found in France or other parts of Europe. Though feared, and with reason, as an international revolutionary menace to the Old Regime, the France of Thermidor and the Directory was in a "reactionary" phase. Persons who called themselves democrats were dubbed anarchists by French officials. "Jacobins" in France were watched by the police, and the Jacobin Club was closed. French soldiers in Holland were ordered to keep away from the Dutch clubs. Dutch radicals were well to the left of the French Republic.

The conflicts that divided the Netherlands were Dutch conflicts, arising from Dutch conditions. The near-unanimity with which the Batavian Republic was first proclaimed merely concealed differences which soon emerged. There were no parties, and no pre-eminent personal leaders, but groupings were numerous and fluctuating, and crisscrossed by social, provincial, and religious lines. The populace, or "masses," politically unawakened, were inclined to be Orangist but could be aroused against the old regents. Artisans and mechanics, shopkeepers and innkeepers, grocers and printers' devils, formed the strength of the democratic or "Jacobin" clubs. They actually believed that people like themselves should enter the government. Described by the French as *véritables sans-culottes,* they were especially strong in the provinces of Holland and Utrecht. Many upper-class people were, in effect, democrats also, using the concepts of Liberty, Equality, and Fraternity, of popular sovereignty, or of the nation one and indivisible, to overthrow the old privileged interests. They included professional men, intellectuals, and many persons of wealth and leisure; the democratic leader, Vreede, was a millionaire, and Gogel, another, remained the financial expert of Holland for many years. Such people welcomed support from the clubs but generally denied being influenced by them. Then there was the great middling stratum who wanted both liberty and order and whom lawlessness or violence would throw immediately toward the right. There were the old regent families, ejected from office and emoluments but not otherwise molested; since there was almost no emigration, they stayed in the country, some accepting certain features of the new order, some going out of politics, and some conspiring with Orange and British agents. In the so-called "land" provinces, inland from the sea there was a preponderantly Orangist gentry. Farthest to the right, so to speak, was the House of Orange. The eldest son or Hereditary Prince—who in 1814 became the first king of the Netherlands—believed from the beginning that some compromise with the revolution should be made. The father, William V, aloof in England, refused any concession whatever. He threw himself humbly on England and Prussia, entreating the king of Prussia, who was his brother-in-law, "to restore the constitution which Your Majesty and His Britannic Majesty deigned to guarantee in 1788."

All issues came together into one—whether the new Batavian Republic should be a unitary or a federal state. The bitterness of this conflict amazed even the French, though they had faced something like it in their own revolution, both in 1789 and in the dispute between the Gironde and the Mountain. A Dutchman explained to Noël, the French envoy, that "there had been less of a gulf to fill between monarchism and republicanism in France than exists here between federalism and unity." The formal constitutional question expressed social realities. Democrats were unitarists, conservatives were federalists: the correlation was almost perfect. In fact, the radical clubs, after January 1795, commonly changed their name to societies of *Eenen Ondeelbarheit*, or "One and Indivisible" clubs. Noël caught on quickly. "It is obvious," he wrote home, "that the families which, under the monstrous system of sovereignty for each province, each town, were able to perpetuate themselves in offices which became hereditary for them are not inclined to fuse all these sovereigns into one."

Federalism, or decentralization, the letting of each town and province alone, thus came to stand for "feudalism," for the old patriciates and oligarchies, with closed magistracies and self-perpetuating councils, for the corporative and ecclesiastical society, the *Ständestaat*, and also for the clumsy and slow-moving administrative machinery which even conservatives admitted to require some reform. The unitary, solid state, in which the old entities should be abolished, meant uniform rights for all persons considered as individuals, and it meant the sovereignty of the people one and indivisible, which in turn was a legalistic way of saying that neither family, nor church, nor estate, nor town council, nor provincial assembly possessed any public power in its own right. There was also the matter of the public debt of the province of Holland. For two centuries Holland had kept the confederation going by its own inordinate contributions. Its debt was enormous, larger than the debt of the Bourbon monarchy in 1789. In a unitary state this debt would become the debt of a so-called "Batavian nation"—an uninviting prospect outside Holland, especially among the squires of the land provinces, who had never much approved the financial and maritime goings-on of the Hollanders anyway. . . .

After much backing and filling, amending and patching, an admittedly compromise constitution was submitted to the voters in August 1797. This itself was a revolutionary step. Neither the constitution of the United States, nor most of the American state constitutions, nor the French constitution of 1789–91 had had to face the hazards of popular ratification. Many Dutch leaders, as well as Noël and the French Directory, hoped desperately for approval. They felt that any constituted government was better than none. Nevertheless, the voters rejected it overwhelmingly, by 108,761 to 27,955 votes. The constitution clearly failed because it was too much of a compromise and so satisfied no party of any strength. It was rejected in every province. In populous Holland and Utrecht, where unitary democrats were strong, it was the democrats who voted against it; in the eastern or land provinces, the federalists and conservatives. Both parties hoped to do better on a new draft.

Thus in August 1797, almost three years after the revolution, the Batavian Republic still had no government. The old order had collapsed, leaving only a vacuum. The revolutionaries in the broad sense of the word—men of all political stripes who were willing to take the antihereditary oath—were unable to agree and unwilling to compromise. . . .

Events of the late summer of 1797 are best considered from an all-European point of view. It was a time of reviving counterrevolutionary hopes and of apprehension among friends of the new order. Elections in France had recently brought a majority of the royalist and peace party into the French legislative chambers. If this group got control of the French government, reaction could be expected in France, and the spread of revolution in Italy under Bonaparte could be stopped. Dutch conservatives took hope in the rejection of the Dutch constitution—which was a step, in their minds, toward a settlement more to their liking. It was known that French *émigrés*, royalists, Orange emissaries, spies, and British agents were everywhere active. Rightist coups were expected.

What happened, however, was the French coup d'état of Fructidor, on September 4, 1797. Republicans in France combined with Bonaparte to suppress counterrevolution. They purged the French chambers and Directory, thus for a time giving encouragement to the democratic left. The Dutch democrats were delighted. As one of them wrote from Amsterdam to his colleague, Professor Valckenaer, "If the plans of the [French] royalists had only succeeded, how fast Father William [i.e., William V] would have been with his! We have been finding this citizen's agents all over the country. Six of them were arrested yesterday in this city.". . .

After rejecting the constitution, the Dutch elected a new convention to draft another. Moderates were weaker, and democrats stronger, than in the first; but still no majority could be formed to agree upon anything. On October 11 came the battle of Camperdown. The Dutch fleet was defeated by the British. For the first time in history a Dutch admiral was taken captive. This turn of events discredited the provisional governing committees. Patriots believed that moderates in the government had deliberately ordered out the fleet before the time called for in the Franco-Batavian war plan, in order to avoid making a true contribution to the impending invasion of Ireland. The cry was renewed for a unitary and effectual government that would not mismanage the navy.

The Dutch clubs and other radicals demanded a Dutch Fructidor. They asked for the recall of Noël, who they said had mixed too much with "aristocrats." The French post-Fructidorian government, having broken off peace talks with England, was committed to a renewal of hostilities and preparing to invade the British Isles. It was losing patience with the interminable Dutch indecision and prepared to support any strong government that would act as an ally. The Fructidor turnover brought Talleyrand to the foreign ministry. His predecessor, Charles Delacroix (father of the painter Eugène Delacroix), went to Holland to replace Noël. Delacroix was an old Jacobin, who had voted for the death of Louis XVI; he was a man of experience and recognized ability, who had been chief assistant to Turgot years before and was to end his life as one of Napoleon's prefects. According to his present instructions, his first duty was to get a workable constitution adopted in the Netherlands; the matter should preferably be left to the Dutch, and honest elections were to be desired, but if necessary to get a decision, the elections might be "fixed.". . .

Delacroix brought with him a draft constitution, put together by both French and Dutch hands, and retouched in Paris by Merlin de Douai and Barras. This constitution, or something like it, he had to get accepted by the Dutch convention, which therefore had to be purged. Forty-nine members of the stalemated convention—about a third of the whole—reached an understanding with him. They submitted to him a long document, entitled "Constitutional points agreed upon," and listing the articles of a "democratic, representative constitution." They agreed to exclude forcibly those of their fellow-members "in known opposition to the principles here announced.". . .

The coup d'état took place on January 22, 1798. Twenty-two members were driven from the assembly. The re-formed constitutional committee considered Delacroix's draft, which it felt no obligation to accept blindly. In fact, it did not find the draft democratic enough. Small Holland now gave revolutionary lessons to its mighty neighbor. The Dutch, as the committee explained to Delacroix, were "capable of a greater measure of democracy than would be suitable for the French." They proposed more direct election by original voters (i.e., less power to electoral colleges), procedures for amendment by popular initiative, and modification of the bicameral provision to keep aristocrats from dominating the upper chamber. Delacroix accepted these suggestions.

The resulting constitution, agreed to by the purged convention, was unitary and democratic. It extinguished the old provinces and replaced them with eight "departments" of equal population, whose frontiers bore no relation to the old provincial borders. It granted manhood suffrage except to persons receiving public relief. It consolidated the debt and the revenues. It abolished all guilds, monopolies, and other barriers to the circulation of persons and goods, and it completed the disestablishment of the Reformed religion. It provided for a bicameral legislature and for a collegiate executive of five directors to supervise the ministries, as in France. In general, while closely resembling the French constitution of 1795, it represented a trend toward somewhat more democracy, on the one hand, and toward a stronger executive, on the other.

This constitution, submitted for popular ratification in April 1798, was overwhelmingly adopted by a vote of 165,520 to 11,597. Pressure was brought at the polls, where the antiheredity oath was again exacted. It is to be noted, however, that almost half the adult males, or almost 10 per cent of the aggregate population, actually voted—at this time less than half the adult males of Virginia and Massachusetts possessed even the right to vote; and thirty years later, in the famous Jacksonian "revolution" in the United States, no more than 10 per cent of the total white population actually went to the polls. The best evidence that the constitution suited a great majority of the Dutch people is the fact that, when the democrats themselves were driven from power, their democratic constitution was retained. It remained in effect until replaced by the Bonapartist constitution of 1801, which modified only a few of its principles. Unity, consolidation, equality of civil rights, and religious disestablishment remained permanent. As the Dutch say of their work of 1798, they took the medicine but threw away the bottle.

It was the behavior of the democrats rather than the democratic constitution that led to further discord. They did nothing really drastic; there was no attempt at social revolution, general confiscation, or terror. They did, however, take steps to secure themselves in power. On the advice of Delacroix and remembering the precedent of the French Convention in 1795, the Dutch Convention enacted a "two-thirds" rule, requiring that two-thirds of the members of new legislative chambers should be former members of the purged convention. This self-perpetuating action aroused general indignation. There was also a general scramble for office; the unitary central government, using its newly acquired powers, put all sorts of democrats into local jobs. It was called a purge but was not altogether different from the American democratic practice of "rotation." What was more serious, and justified only by the familiar argument of defense against reaction, the Dutch democrats also tried to purge the voters, by excluding political rivals from the polls. . . .

It is probably true that the Dutch regime set up on January 22, giving a good deal of room to the really common people, though supported by men of substance, did not offer a basis on which the politically significant classes could reach stable agreement. The men who controlled the Dutch finances and the Dutch navy withheld their support. The French government still wanted an effectual ally. Delacroix, the old Jacobin, earnestly defended the military usefulness of the Dutch regime to France. Where the preceding Dutch rulers had done nothing but get the fleet knocked to pieces at Camperdown, the present Dutch government, he wrote in May 1798, maintained twelve ships of the line and transport for 15,000 troops and had assembled 230 vessels at Dunkirk to embark the right wing of the French *Armée d'Angleterre*. But, unknown to Delacroix, in May Bonaparte sailed for Egypt to assail Britain in the East; the French, while still needing Dutch power in northern waters, postponed the project of invasion. In May, also, the French government veered in an antidemocratic direction; the French elections of 1798, having shown a revival of Jacobinism, were quashed by the so-called coup d'état of Floréal. Talleyrand and the French Directors allowed Gogel, Daendels, and other Dutch leaders, in agreement with the French military commander in Holland and with one of Delacroix's own civilian subordinates, to form a conspiracy against Delacroix and the existing Dutch regime. Dutch politics, if not dictated, were certainly shaped by the French: the Dutch Fructidor was followed by the Dutch Floréal, which, in turn, foreshadowed the French Brumaire.

On June 12, 1798, by a new coup d'état, General Daendels arrested the leading members of the Batavian government and dissolved the chambers. Delacroix left Holland a week later. He submitted to Talleyrand a final report on his mission, justifying his own and the Dutch democrats' actions. The coup of June 12 looked to him like military dictatorship. "May the excessive ease with which it was carried out not persuade some obscure centurion that to win all he need only dare all!". . .

. . . As late as 1806 the British Whig, Sir John Carr, who managed to travel in Napoleonic Europe by posing as an American and who spoke some Dutch, insisted that the Dutch were amazingly content under King Louis Bonaparte. . . .

The Dutch revolution of 1795, Pieter Geyl has said, "was a true revolution, in the sense that it created a new government, a new order, and a new law." It was also a typical revolution of the era, according to the view taken in this paper, that is, it reveals, on a small and well-lit stage, a great many phenomena then common to western Europe and in some degree the Western world. It was not imported from France, though it made use of French power. It was initiated by a small minority, but this is not to say that this minority worked against an unwilling majority, or that any majority existed at all, or that other equally identifiable minorities were not equally small. No special theories, drawn from Taine and Marx, are necessary to explain the Dutch Jacobins. Indeed, as we have seen, Dutch conservatives in 1794 harbored "Jacobin" ideas, to suppress disaffection by force, to control the flight of capital, to raise a citizen army: all governments since 1794 have done the same, as the price of survival. It is clear also that Catholics might make active revolutionists, depending upon conditions. The internal dynamics of revolution, or push and pull between left and right, are well illustrated by the Dutch example, which suggests that immovability on the part of older authorities, by discouraging compromise, may throw moderates into dependence upon the left and so produce more "radicalism" than radicals could ever produce alone. It is clear that democracy was at issue; the term was no smear-word; it was sensibly used by democrats and antidemocrats alike. National unity was also at issue; but unity and indivisibility, *een- en ondeelbarheit,* when applied to this tiny country, need raise no specter of militant nationalism: it meant only the merging of an old class and church-oriented society into a new civic community. It is evident also that the world war which began in 1792, and especially the war between France and Great Britain, while ideological issues were dependent on its outcome, was by no means ideological alone, nor a war of offense and defense with respect to revolution. It was a part of the hundred-year-old resistance of continental Europeans to the rise of the British empire. Not merely did revolutionary sympathy make men anti-British. Existing anti-British sentiment, due to the rise of the British empire and sea power, might, conversely, incline them to sympathy with revolution. The British government might have won more allies in defending Europe from revolution, had it been more disinterested—a thought not inapplicable to Americans today. Finally, these Dutch events suggest that if only the whole revolutionary and counterrevolutionary movement, for Europe and America in these years, could be put together in one story, it would at least be very interesting—if not hopelessly entangled—and might even give us a better understanding of what has really happened in our world in the last two hundred years.

The American Revolution Considered as a Social Movement: A Re-evaluation

FREDERICK B. TOLLES

Frederick B. Tolles, professor of Quaker history at Swarthmore College, has been chiefly interested in American social and intellectual history of the eighteenth century. He made his reputation with his book *Meeting House and Counting House: Quaker Merchants of Colonial Philadelphia* (1948), which has been followed by biographical studies of two members of an outstanding Philadelphia Quaker family, the Logans. In the following article, Professor Tolles is concerned with the broader social changes which characterized the revolutionary era.

SOMETIMES a single essay, a monograph, or a series of lectures makes historiographical history. It was so in 1893 when Frederick Jackson Turner read his paper on "The Significance of the Frontier in American History." It was so again in 1913 when Charles A. Beard published his *Economic Interpretations of the Constitution.* And it was so in 1925 when J. Franklin Jameson delivered his four lectures at Princeton on "The American Revolution Considered as a Social Movement."

At first glance the comparison with Turner and Beard may seem strained. We are accustomed to think of Jameson as a scholar's scholar, a kind of indispensable historical midwife—curator and editor of manuscripts, director of other men's research, editor of the *American Historical Review*—not as a pathbreaker, an innovator. But this is to do him less than justice. *The American Revolution Considered as a Social Movement* stands as a landmark in recent American historiography, a slender but unmistakable signpost, pointing a new direction for historical research and interpretation. Before Jameson, the American Revolution had been a chapter in political, diplomatic, and military history, a story of Faneuil Hall and Lexington, Independence Hall and Valley Forge, Versailles and Yorktown. After Jameson, it became something different, something greater—a seismic disturbance in American society, a sudden quickening in the American mind.

The American Revolution, like the French, Jameson believed, was accompanied by social and cultural changes of profound significance.

> The stream of revolution, once started, could not be confined within narrow banks, but spread abroad upon the land. Many economic desires, many social aspirations were set free by the political struggle, many aspects of colonial society profoundly altered by the forces thus let loose. The relations of social classes to each other, the institution of slavery, the

From Frederick B. Tolles, "The American Revolution Considered as a Social Movement: A Re-evaluation," *The American Historical Review,* LX (1954), 1–12. Reprinted by permission of *The American Historical Review.*

system of landholding, the course of business, the forms and spirit of the intellectual and religious life, all felt the transforming hand of revolution, all emerged from under it in shapes advanced many degrees nearer to those we know.

No more than Turner's or Beard's was Jameson's notion wholly new. Just a year earlier, in his massive volume on *The American States during and after the Revolution,* Allan Nevins had devoted fifty pages to the task of demonstrating in impressive detail that "a social and intellectual revolution" occurred between Lexington and Yorktown. Nearly twenty years before, Carl Becker had described the Revolution as a twofold contest: for home-rule on the one hand, for "the democratization of American politics and society" on the other. As far back as 1787, Benjamin Rush had perceived that the American revolution was bigger than the American war, that the real revolution was in "the principles, morals, and manners of our citizens," and that, far from being over, that revolution had only begun.

Jameson's view of the Revolution was not new, but no one hitherto had marshaled the evidence so compactly, conveyed it so lucidly, or argued from it so persuasively. Perceptive historians immediately greeted his little volume as a gem of historical writing—"a truly notable book," Charles A. Beard called it," . . . cut with a diamond point to a finish, studded with novel illustrative materials, gleaming with new illumination, serenely engaging in style, and sparingly garnished with genial humor."

The influence of this little book with the long title has grown steadily. A year after its publication, the Beards summarized its thesis in their widely read *Rise of American Civilization.* Jameson's emphasis on social factors harmonized perfectly with the intellectual and political climate of the 1930's. In 1940, after the author's death, a second edition appeared, and in 1950 a third—an unusual tribute to a set of academic lectures. With the passage of a quarter-century, the book has achieved the standing of a minor classic. One will find hardly a textbook that does not paraphrase or quote Jameson's words, borrow his illustrations, cite him in its bibliography. The notion of the Revolution as a social upheaval has achieved the final seal of acceptance: it has been taken over by the historical novelists—by such writers as Kenneth Roberts and Howard Fast, to name two rather unlikely bedfellows.

Jameson, one suspects, had no idea he was writing a classic. His aim was simply to challenge American historians by opening new windows on the Revolutionary era, suggesting new directions for future research, throwing out tentative hypotheses for others to test. Over the past quarter-century historians have risen to his challenge with a flood of articles, monographs, academic dissertations, and full-dress histories bearing on one or another of his propositions. But the average textbook-writer, one is tempted to believe, has not got beyond Jameson. The time has come to go back and ask how Jameson's original thesis stands up in the light of all this detailed research; what modifications, if any, must be made; what further extensions, if any, are possible.

Jameson disposed his arguments under four rubrics—the status of persons, the land, industry and commerce, thought and feeling. If we recognize, as he did, that such divisions are purely arbitrary, we may adopt his procedure.

American society, he suggested, was measurably democratized during the Revolution. The upper stratum, the old colonial aristocracy, was largely liquidated—by banishment, voluntary exile, or impoverishment. New groups rose to the surface to take their places. "In most states the strength of the revolutionary party lay most largely in the plain people," and the social changes which they brought about naturally tended "in the direction of levelling democracy." Broadening of the suffrage elevated "whole classes of people . . . in their social status," and the revolutionary philosophy of liberty wrought improvements in the condition of the most debased class in America—the Negro slaves.

Recent studies of individual states and regions seem to suggest that Jameson was too sweeping when he equated colonial aristocrats with Loyalists and implied that this group was erased from American society. In eastern Massachusetts it was perhaps true that "a majority of the old aristocracy" emigrated. But in the central and western part of the state the oldest, most respected families chose the Whig side and remained to perpetuate their local rule in the days of the early Republic. In New Hampshire, except around Portsmouth, society had never been highly stratified, and the Tory emigration bore away few outstanding individuals. In Connecticut, where "the native aristocracy of culture, wealth, religion, and politics" tended to be loyal to the crown, at least half of the Tories never left the state. Others were welcomed back even before the war was over. Within six months of the peace treaty, New Haven was openly extending an invitation to former Loyalists to return, and President Ezra Stiles of Yale College was grumbling about efforts "silently to bring the Tories into an Equality and Supremacy among the Whigs." In New York and Philadelphia, many prominent merchants—perhaps the majority—were Loyalists, or at least "neutralists," and they stayed on in such numbers as to give a definite tone to postwar society, politics, and business in these important centers. In Maryland, the "internal" Revolution turns out to have been a struggle between one group of aristocrats—planters, merchants, lawyers—and another; the "plain people" took little part in the conflict and the resultant social shifts were minimal. In Virginia, of course, most of the "F.F.V.'s" were Whigs, and their control of politics was to continue through the days of the "Virginia dynasty." In the North Carolina back country it was the "plain people"—the old Regulators—who were most stubbornly Loyalist. Clearly Jameson's generalizations about the fate of the old aristocracy must be qualified.

What about the new democracy of the Revolutionary period? Unquestionably a sense of dignity and importance came to the common man—the small farmer, the town artisan—as a result of his revolutionary activities and the limited extension of the suffrage. But before we can say with assurance how democratic the new society was, we must answer the prior question: how undemocratic was the old? No one will dispute the fact that provincial society was stratified, that class distinctions existed, that political and social equality were hardly dreamed of. A recent brilliant study of electoral practices in colonial Massachusetts raises, however, some questions. By means of ingenious statistical methods and samplings of contemporary opinion, the author of this study has shown rather convincingly that, in the Bay Colony at least, practically all adult males had the vote. Massachusetts society before 1776, he concludes, was "very close to a complete democracy." And he hints of further revisions to come. "As for the 'internal revolution' in other colonies," he says, "—perhaps we should take another look. There is more than a hint in the records that what applies to Massachusetts applies without too much change to other colonies as well."

Though the Negro slave received some indirect benefits from the Revolution, the indentured servant, Jameson found, received none. Nor has subsequent research uncovered any important evidence that he overlooked. While he was dwelling on the negative side, Jameson might have mentioned another large dependent class that gained nothing in status as a result of the Revolution. Even before independence was declared, that doughty feminist Abigail Adams was writing to her husband in Congress: "By the way, in the new code of laws which I suppose it will be necessary for you to make, I desire you would remember the ladies and be more generous and favorable to them than your ancestors." Her husband wrote back as much in earnest as in jest: "Depend on it, we know better than to repeal our masculine systems." It was to be nearly three quarters of a century before the Declaration of Independence would be revised by a group of determined ladies at Seneca Falls to read: "All men and women are created equal." Both negative and positive evidence, then, suggests that the Revolution made less difference in the status of persons in America than Jameson believed.

The doctrine that underlies Jameson's second lecture is, quite explicitly, economic determinism: "political democracy," he says flatly, "came to the United States as a result of economic democracy." The movement for manhood suffrage which reached its fruition in Jacksonian America, he maintains, was rooted in a peculiarly American type of land tenure—the system of small holdings or what he chooses to call "peasant proprietorship." This system the Revolution fixed upon the nation when it swept away the royal restrictions, the archaic manorial laws and usages which had encumbered the land throughout the colonial period. There was, he makes clear, "no violent outbreak," no bloody massacre of landlords as in France a decade later. Still, "in a quiet, sober, Anglo-Saxon way a great change was reflected in the land system of America between the years 1775 and 1795." Specifically, the changes were of three sorts: the discontinuance of quitrents and of the king's right to mast-trees, the abolition of primogeniture and entail, the confiscation and distribution of the Tory estates.

The importance of the quitrents and the king's "broad arrow" was probably more symbolic than real. Jameson himself admitted this: payment of quitrents, he pointed out, was "largely evaded"; the law giving the king's surveyors the right to reserve the tallest, straightest pine trees for the Royal Navy "was not rigorously enforced." Still, no historian will deny the importance of an emotion-laden symbol, and Jameson insists, quite rightly, that the quitrent and the king's "broad arrow" were symbols of an obsolete and alien feudalism, that until they were done away with, private property was not private property.

There is high authority, of course, for attaching great significance to the abolition of primogeniture and entail in Virginia—the authority of Thomas Jefferson. But these gestures too, it now appears, were more important in the realm of symbol than of economic reality. In point of fact, neither primogeniture nor entail operated to any important degree in Virginia. Recent research has shown that most estates in the Old Dominion were not entailed but could be freely alienated. And primogeniture was mandatory only if the property-owner died intestate. Most Virginia planters were careful to make wills. By their wills they often distributed their property among all their sons, and sometimes even their daughters. So Jefferson, in the words of his most authoritative biographer, "did not destroy the country gentry as a group with the blows of his mighty ax, and there is insufficient reason to believe that he wanted to." What he did was merely to "remove legal vestiges of Old World aristocracy." The sweeping conclusion reached by a recent student of this problem in Virginia may well apply to other colonies: "No radical change of custom in devising estates resulted from the abolition of primogeniture and entail."

On the confiscation of Loyalist lands much has been written of late years. The evidence has not been canvassed for all the states, but a definite conclusion seems to be emerging that considerably less diffusion and democratization of landownership resulted from the breakup of these estates and their disposition in small parcels than Jameson supposed.

The most intensive study has been centered on the southern counties of New York, where the DeLanceys, the Bayards, the Philipses held sway in colonial times over their vast baronies. When the revolutionary New York government seized the estates and sold them off, some of the land, to be sure, went to former tenants and other landless individuals. But the bulk of it was bought up by wealthy patriots and merely augmented the domains of rival families like the Livingstons, Schuylers, and Roosevelts. "While it is true," concludes the author of this study, "that the disposal of the loyalist estates effected a greater diffusion of ownership, it is questionable whether it went far toward a radical redistribution of landed wealth and a new social and economic order."

The same thing seems to have been true in Maryland, where wealthy Whig planters and speculators bought up a large proportion of the desirable Tory lands in Baltimore and Frederick counties. Nor is the story greatly different in western Massachusetts or New Hampshire. The South Carolina confiscation law, in the opinion of a contemporary, was actually "so framed that a man who wants land has no chance to get any," for the state required security which only the wealthy landowner could provide.

The case of North Carolina is instructive. The authority on the Loyalists of that state, noting that the confiscated lands were sold in plots averaging two hundred acres, concludes with Jameson that the confiscations "tended to make the Revolution economic and social as well as political." From his own evidence, however, one could draw the equally justified inference that many a wealthy patriot took advantage of the bargain prices to increase his holdings and consequently his social status. The largest Tory estate was that of the great speculator Henry McCulloh—some 40,000 acres. Of the ninety purchasers of McCulloh's lands thirty-four bought more than one tract. Some acquired as many as ten or fifteen, thereby creating estates as large as 5,000 acres. Robert Raiford purchased parcels from five different Tories and put together an estate of more than a thousand acres. The 3,600-acre estate of Thomas Hooper passed almost intact to John McKinsey. Before a final generalization can be made about the social effects of the confiscations in North Carolina, we need to know more about the previous economic status of the purchasers.

The largest estate to be confiscated in America, as Jameson pointed out, was that of the Penn family. By the Divesting Act of 1779 the Pennsylvania legislature assumed control of twenty-one and a half million acres—all the ungranted lands which by royal charter had belonged to the proprietors. But this proprietary land, from which the Penns had never received any income, was comparable, surely, to the ungranted crown lands which fell into the hands of the other commonwealths. Much more significant is the fact that the private manors, the "proprietary tenths," of the Penns, amounting to more than 500,000 acres, together with the quitrents on them, were specifically "confirmed, ratified and established for ever" in the hands of the Penn family—and this by the most "radical" of all the revolutionary legislatures!

Clearly, there are two ways of reading the evidence concerning the confiscation and sale of Loyalist lands. Jameson, who was arguing a thesis, chose to stress the "democratizing" effects. But there were other social consequences of an opposite tendency—the aggrandizement of certain individuals and families already well entrenched, the opportunities opened for speculation—and we shall not understand all the social results of this great sequestration of lands until we assess these as well.

In particular, until someone has studied the social effects of land speculation in the Revolutionary and post-Revolutionary era as Professor Paul W. Gates has done for a later period, we shall not know whether the operations of the speculators hastened or delayed settlement, encouraged or hindered the system of small holdings. Meanwhile, we may note that Professor Abernethy considers the Virginia land office act of 1779 (drafted, incidentally, by Thomas Jefferson) "a colossal mistake," a blow to economic democracy, and a retarding influence on settlement because it played into the hands of speculators and thus *prevented* the diffusion of land in small holdings. By this act, he says, "democracy was defeated in Virginia at the moment when it might have had its birth."

Land speculation was, of course, a form of business enterprise. And business enterprise, it is now clear, took a sharp spurt as a direct result of Revolutionary conditions. That Jameson should have perceived and stressed this in 1925 is sufficiently remarkable. His chapter on "Industry and Commerce" undoubtedly opened the eyes of many American historians to the economic facts which, as everyone now recognizes, are as crucial in the history of a war as the political, diplomatic, and military facts.

Some of the new economic paths which the Revolution opened, turned out to be blind alleys. Postwar interest in the improvement of agriculture, reflected in the sudden popularity of farmers' societies, proved to be short-lived and relatively ineffectual. In some regions the wartime growth of manufacturing, which Jameson noted, was choked off by the postwar flood of cheap British goods, which he neglected to mention.

But in other ways enterprise burgeoned and flourished under wartime and postwar conditions. Opportunities for quick gains in privateering and profiteering, the opening of new markets, the expansion of the credit system, the injection of new supplies of specie into the economy as a result of foreign borrowing, the rise of new business groups around men like Jeremiah Wadsworth, William Duer, Robert Morris, the very idea (a new one for Americans) of large-scale business association—all these were constructive economic forces generated by the Revolution. Especially important were the rise of banking and the spread of incorporation. In the words of one economic historian, the Bank of North America, which opened in Philadelphia in 1782, "was identified with the American Revolutionary 'settlement,'—as the Bank of England was with that of the Glorious Revolution."

The same scholar gives us some revealing statistics on the chartering of business corporations: "In contrast with the half-dozen American business charters granted in the entire colonial period, eleven were issued in the United States between 1781 and 1785, twenty-two between 1786 and 1790, and 114 between 1791 and 1795." Economic facts of this order have led one writer to treat the American Revolution as "the triumph of American mercantile capitalism." Whether or not one wishes to adopt this view, it is clear, as Jameson dimly perceived, that the Revolution loosed potent new forces in the American economy. How these forces were related to the social and political democracy which Jameson saw as products of the Revolution remains to be studied.

When he turned from the hard facts of economic history to the impalpable realm of "thought and feeling," Jameson was less at home. Yet even here he opened vistas which a generation of intellectual and cultural historians have explored with profit. The greater part of his final lecture is concerned with the effect of independence on the churches—with disestablishment and the separation of church and state, with the reorganization of the churches on a national basis, with the wartime decline of religious life and the postwar spread of liberal theologies. Subsequent research has added little to Jameson's account of these matters, except to fill in details. What Jameson did—and it was no trifling achievement—was to bring American church history within the purview of American historians—to take, as it were, the first steps toward giving this neglected orphan child a home and a standing within the family of historical disciplines.

Certain of his insights, naturally, have proved more fruitful than others. His *obiter dictum* to the effect that military men can never again play the part in public life that they played after the Revolution falls strangely on our ears, who have known the proconsulate of MacArthur, the foreign ministry of Marshall, the Presidency of Eisenhower. Curiously, Jameson found little evidence of educational advance in the Revolutionary era, except for the founding of new colleges. Had he taken a broader view of education, he might have recognized a number of important developments directly or indirectly related to wartime experience: the improvement of medicine (including dentistry) and of medical education; the emergence of civil engineering from military engineering; the founding of Judge Tapping Reeve's "law school" at Litchfield, Connecticut, in 1784; the diffusion of scientific knowledge through the revived activity of the American Philosophical Society and the founding of the American Academy of Arts and Sciences; the popularity of pamphleteering as a form of mass education; and —not least important—the informal education, the widening of horizons, that resulted from wartime mobility, from the fact that, for the first time, many Americans rubbed elbows—and minds—not only with Europeans but with other Americans. The school of intellectual and cultural historians which has sprung up in the last quarter century has made much of the "intellectual democracy" and the "cultural nationalism" which Jameson vaguely perceived as concomitants, in the realm of "thought and feeling," of the American Revolution.

The danger here as elsewhere is that the historian, misled by his enthusiasm for the concept of "revolution," will posit too abrupt a set of changes, will pay too little attention to the evidences of historical continuity. Jameson himself did not altogether avoid this pitfall. For example, he wrote that "Joel Barlow's *Vision of Columbus,* or President Stile's celebrated election sermon on *The United States Elevated to Glory and Honor,* could not possibly have been written twenty years earlier." If he meant by this that the idea of the United States as an independent nation was not entertained in the 1760's, the statement is obviously correct, though hardly startling. If he meant that before 1775 no American felt or expressed love for the land, pride in its people, confidence in its future, he was just as obviously wrong. For one finds strong feelings of American patriotism in a pre-Revolutionary poem like Freneau and Brackenridge's "The Rising Glory of America," written in 1771, in the sermons of Samuel Davies and Jonathan Mayhew in the 1750's, even in Judge Samuel Sewall's proud paean to his beloved Plum Island, Crane Pond, and Turkey Hill as far back as the last decade of the seventeenth century. Indeed the points at which the supports to Jameson's thesis seem weakest—where for example he argues for sharper changes in the political and social status of individuals than can be justified on the evidence—are precisely those points at which he overlooked or underestimated dynamic forces already present in the society of late colonial America.

Still, a historian who fashions so useful a conceptual tool, who popularizes so fruitful a hypothesis, who enlarges so notably our understanding of a significant era in American history, can be forgiven a few oversights, a few overstatements. Basically, the "Jameson thesis" is still sound, and, what is more important, still vital and suggestive, capable of still further life, still greater usefulness. Jameson, after all, did much more than give us a new approach to the American Revolution. He formulated and cogently applied to a particular period an important general thesis—"the thesis that all the varied activities of men in the same country and period have intimate relations with each other, and that one cannot obtain a satisfactory view of any one of them by considering it apart from the others." For this he deserves homage as one of the founders of American social and cultural history.

The Place of the American Revolution in the Causal Pattern of the French Revolution

LOUIS GOTTSCHALK

Louis Gottschalk, professor of modern history at the University of Chicago and a former president of the American Historical Association, has qualifications unique for discussing the relationship between the American and French Revolutions. He has not only earned a distinguished reputation as an authority on the French Revolution, but as the biographer of a definitive life of Lafayette Professor Gottschalk has dealt exhaustively with a hero who has symbolized the links between revolutionary America and France.

On July 4, 1948, the people of the United States will celebrate the 172nd anniversary of the Declaration of Independence. In other words, it is now almost *twice* four score and seven years ago that "our fathers brought forth on this continent a new nation conceived in liberty and dedicated to the proposition that all men are created equal." And we have just finished—in fact, it may be said that we are still engaged in—a great struggle "testing whether that nation or any nation so conceived and so dedicated can long endure."

The principle of liberty and the proposition that all men are created equal were inherited by the people of the United States from a long tradition. That tradition had Biblical origins; its genealogy can easily be traced by the brilliant pattern it weaves through the history of British and European political philosophy and constitutional practice. Its collateral American lines reached maturity in the constitutions of the separate states (some of which came even before the Declaration of Independence), the Declaration of Independence itself, and in the first ten amendments of the federal constitution.

It is sometimes believed that it was because of the principles for which the Americans fought and which they had incorporated in their widely admired Declaration of Independence that the government of France joined with the young American nation to fight against the tyranny symbolized by the British army and its Hessian mercenaries. That belief, however, contains sentimental overtones that do not ring true. That the ideals of "life, liberty and the pursuit of happiness" had a significant influence in determining French foreign policy before 1778, if it is true at all, is true only in small part. How little truth there is in it can be shown by citing the outstanding contemporary French writers on political theory, the very people whose purpose it should have been to promote the ideals of liberty among the French.

From Louis Gottschalk, "The Place of the American Revolution in the Causal Pattern of the French Revolution," *Publications of The American Friends of Lafayette,* No. 2 (Easton, 1948), pp. 495–510. Reprinted by permission of The American Friends of Lafayette.

Take, for example, Beaumarchais. He was one of the writers in the period before the French Revolution largely responsible for the spread of the idea of liberty in France. He was greatly interested in American independence, and was influential in forming the American policy of the French minister of foreign affairs, the Comte de Vergennes. Yet from the letters that Beaumarchais wrote to the minister before 1778, it is clear that he did not intend the ideal of liberty to have the foremost part in that policy. He made the more practical plea that the independence of the American colonies from England would redress the world's commercial balance and would be to the political advantage of the French empire.

And Turgot, also a minister of the king and justly reputed to be one of the outstanding economic reformers of his day, was still less a champion of American freedom. When the minister of foreign affairs sent around a memorandum asking for opinions as to whether the French government should take part in the War of American Independence, Turgot replied: "It seems to me that the most desirable outcome from the viewpoint of the two crowns [the French and the Spanish] would be that England overcome the resistance of her colonies." He went on to say that a long-drawn-out war between the British and the American insurgents would be to the advantage of France. A similar point of view was presented by the Abbé de Mably, generally considered one of the most radical political theorists of the day, in an essay entitled *Notre Gloire ou Nos Rèves*. In short, hard-headed considerations regarding the welfare of France were more typical of the attitude of French writers *before* the Declaration of Independence than the sentimental championing of American liberties.

It is sometimes said that many French soldiers came to America before 1778 to fight on behalf of the ideal of liberty. That is supposed to be particularly true of the Marquis de Lafayette. But it can be shown—I have spent many hours and written many pages in the effort to show—that as a matter of fact Lafayette's interest in political ideals, if it existed at all before 1776, was not very keen. Its vigorous growth came only *after* he had enlisted in the American service, and was not a cause of his doing so. It was less spiritual motives—such as escape from frustration, desire for glory, and hatred of the British—that led to his heroic behavior. What was true of Lafayette was *a fortiori* true of other European soldiers who volunteered their services to the American army, and was still more true of those soldiers who went as part of the French army, following the formal Franco-American alliance, to fight under Rochambeau on the side of Washington. The attitude of the French people before or shortly after the Declaration of Independence [that] was known to them is well summed up by Morellet, another of that group of writers of the eighteenth century Enlightenment called "the *philosophes*." In a letter to the British minister Shelburne dated January 5, 1777—i.e., shortly after news of the Declaration of Independence had reached France—Morellet declared that many partisans of America in Paris were less friendly to American liberty than hostile to Great Britain.

Offsetting this prevalent attitude, however, was that of other Frenchmen who thought of America as fighting the cause of mankind. After Benjamin Franklin got to France, he reported a general feeling that America was fighting for the liberty of all in fighting for her own. Franklin, however, is not the best of witnesses in this regard. Naturally he encountered the most pro-American elements, and the less friendly persons he met were not likely to express themselves freely in his presence. And yet Franklin's testimony enables us to note that the news of the Declaration of Independence, which had arrived in France just about a month ahead of him, marked a significant change in French public opinion. While before the end of 1776 the prevailing attitude toward the American rebellion was Anglophobe, by the beginning of 1777 it had become Americanophile.

For a time after 1776—that is to say, between 1776 and the signing of the treaty of alliance of 1778—the official policy and the opinion of a large part of the population was for the most part Anglophobe and not libertarian. Between 1776 and 1778, the pro-American party in France published a periodical entitled *Les Affaires de l'Angleterre et de l'Amérique*. This periodical appeared to be published in the Belgian city of Antwerp. At any rate, that city was indicated on the title page as its place of origin. It probably was printed and published in Paris, but in order to avoid the censorship authorities, who apparently still were unfriendly to American ideals, it was made to appear to come from a foreign country. This newspaper has often been cited as showing the popularity of republican principles in France before 1778, but recent investigation shows that it endeavored to soften the impact of republican principles against a cushion of anti-English arguments rather than to propound republican principles directly and positively. There was at the same time in Paris also a pro-English, anti-American propaganda intended to counteract that of the friends of America. This English propaganda, organized under the guidance of Isaac De Pinto, played upon the widespread antipathy in France to rebellion and reproached the Americans as insurgents.

The Alliance of 1778 changed the picture thoroughly, making official France outwardly, and the greater part of the French people sincerely, friendly to America as well as hostile to England. That alliance was largely, however, the result rather of the fear that the American colonies might become reconciled to the mother country, thereby re-establishing English supremacy upon the seas and overseas, than of France's interest in the ideals set forth in the Declaration of Independence. The English historian W. E. H. Lecky has well summed up the French attitude of that day. The French, he said, were not moved by American liberty, but they were greatly concerned with American independence. After 1778, however, the spirit of liberty grew in France and cemented the friendliness of the people of France toward the people of the United States.

As a general rule, American history textbooks give the impression that what went on in the thirteen transatlantic British colonies from 1778 to 1783 was the major phase of the War of the American Revolution. Nevertheless, to most contemporaries outside of America, that was only a small part of a much bigger war—one that may indeed be called a "world war," if by that phrase is meant a struggle fought all over the world. Only a portion of the total forces involved were engaged in what is now the eastern part of the United States and Canada. Others fought in the West Indies, South America, Africa and Asia, and on the high seas. The total number of land forces under arms in the United States seldom, if ever, reached more than 40,000 on either side. In only one instance did Washington command more than 16,000 men, and that was at Yorktown, where nearly half of them were French. A bigger army in France had constituted one of the most serious threats of invasion that England had ever had to face before 1940, and in Spain another army nearly as large had besieged Gibraltar and invaded Minorca. The fleets that fought in the East and the West Indies sometimes numbered more men than were engaged in the most decisive land battles of the American phase of the conflict.

Eventually nearly every country of Europe was involved directly or indirectly in the war, which was only another in a century-long series that France had been fighting against England for world hegemony. Since the Treaty of 1763, the French had made a vigorous effort to fan the ill-feeling between the American colonies and their mother country into a flame that could be quenched only with blood. After rebellion started, it would probably have resulted in reconciliation between the colonies and England if the French had been willing that it should end in a peaceful manner. Not only did they form an alliance with the United States, they also brought in the Spanish and the Dutch. Before peace was made, a formidable coalition of world powers was lined up against England instead of merely thirteen under-populated colonies.

France also put a great deal of effort and money into the thirteen colonies themselves. True, the forces sent there were small compared to those sent elsewhere. Likewise, the fleets that sailed there went usually on side-trips from their campaigns in the West Indies. But the visit of one of those fleets proved to be the means by which Cornwallis was cut off from aid or retreat, and the half-army that Rochambeau placed under Washington at Yorktown (after agreeing to wait no longer for the other half to come) was the deciding factor in winning that decisive encounter.

Though France, Spain, Holland, and the United States formed quite a strong coalition, they were not the only countries involved in the war. Practically every other big European state was included in a league of "armed neutrality," organized to fight England "short of war" (to use a phrase not then current). They resisted her on the high seas, seeking to refute the contention that she ruled the waves and that the oceans were not free. Thus, Russia, Prussia, the Holy Roman Empire, the Scandinavian countries, Portugal and the Two Sicilies became indirectly involved in the War of American Independence. The separate German states also became interested in its outcome, since Austria and Prussia were carrying on a little war of their own—the so-called "Potato War" (1778–79)—which remained localized and bloodless because England and France, allies of Prussia and Austria respectively, were busily engaged in fighting each other in America and elsewhere. Thus another important aspect of European history during the eighteenth century—the struggle for leadership in the Holy Roman Empire —was for a while affected by what went on in America.

Nor did the war end when the American phase of it was decided. Yorktown was fought in 1781, but peace was not made until 1783. Several things that occurred in the meantime had a greater influence than the victory at Yorktown on what that peace would be. For example, France was decisively defeated in the West Indies waters, and it became obvious that the siege of Gibraltar would not succeed. These failures rather than Yorktown determined the outcome for the Spanish, the Dutch, and the French. They determined also that Britannia would continue to rule the waves, even though she lost her thirteen Continental colonies.

Thus it happened that, from the military and diplomatic point of view, the Revolutionary War was much more than a war for American independence. Although time was to show that the establishment of a sovereign American federation was perhaps the most important result of that war, to contemporaries the future of the United States appeared to be only one among many issues that had induced the big powers to become involved in the struggle. It is even conceivable that if the Battles of Lexington and Concord had not made the American rebellion the immediate occasion of that struggle, England and France might have engaged about the same time anyway in another round of their hundred-year contest for control of the seas and of the colonies beyond the seas. In that event, it is also conceivable, the strategy on both sides might have been much the same as it actually was, except perhaps for the campaigns on the North American continent.

In other words, the War of the American Revolution was a conflict in which France played the major part on the allied side and the American states a minor one. To Frenchmen the capture of small islands like Grenada and Dominica and naval defeats like the Battle of the Saints in the

West Indies were no less important and roused no less enthusiasm or distress than Yorktown. When victory finally was won, Frenchmen rejoiced not so much because the United States was independent as because England had been humbled, her empire torn asunder, and her control of trade and the seas jeopardized.

In 1783, the "Second Hundred Years' War" looked as if it were over and had ended in a decision favorable to France. The conflict was not over, however. The very effort France had made to win the latest bout left her too much exhausted to reap the expected rewards. Exhaustion soon combined with other complications to lead to domestic collapse. Eventually the struggle was renewed, with revolutionary ideologies as one of the weapons in this fight, and came to a close only with the decisive defeat of Napoleon Bonaparte and France.

In preparing that collapse of France with its subsequent revolutionary ideology, the American Revolution played a part that has not always been properly understood, though generally recognized. A few years ago I tried to show that unrest alone is insufficient to create a revolution. In addition, I maintained, there must exist a sense of solidarity among the restless; and they must also have leadership and some program of reform. Even with all these, however, my argument continued, revolutions have been known to fail if they met with effective conservative resistance; and hence it follows that revolutions succeed not so much because the revolutionaries are strong as because the vested interests are weak—or, to use Hegelian terms, not so much because antithesis is irresistible as because thesis has collapsed.

The French Revolution, for example, could hardly have come about without the American Revolution. Unrest, the factor for which one naturally looks first in analyzing the causes of a revolution, would perhaps have been no less pronounced in France if the American Revolution had not occurred. It was caused by many age-old social, economic, political, religious, intellectual, and other provocations, with which the fate of America had very little association. But one important source of dissatisfaction was definitely connected with the American Revolutionary War. While popular uneasiness had been rife for decades, it did not come to a head until the French treasury was threatened with bankruptcy. That danger was in large part due to French sacrifices in the American Revolution. The French had given and loaned great amounts of money to America. They had also made loans to other allies. They had sent huge armies and fleets to every quarter of the globe. The war is generally estimated to have cost France 2,000,000,000 livres. The program of economy and reform that France's comptroller-general, Turgot, had embarked upon before the war had had to be abandoned. Not only were Turgot's sympathizers disillusioned, but also, when the war was over, France's accumulated debt had reached about 4,000,000,000 livres. Meanwhile the cost of living had gone up distressingly.

It is difficult to translate the significance of a 4,000,000,000 livre debt for France of the 1780's into terms that would be intelligible to a twentieth-century American audience. In the first place, our attitude toward national indebtedness has changed, and many, if not most, of us no longer think that having an unfavorable trade balance or being a debtor rather than a creditor nation is necessarily disastrous if the national economy is otherwise sound. In France of the 1780's, however, Adam Smith and his ideas of free trade as the true basis of the wealth of nations were not yet well known, and if the Physiocrats were more renowned, their emphasis was rather upon the virtues of a healthy domestic agriculture than upon those of vigorous international trade and exchange. Hence all but a few in France felt that a large national debt would ruin the country's credit; and that feeling did more to make their fears come true than the logic of the actual situation.

In addition, correctly to appreciate the differences between our reactions and theirs to such a situation, we must make allowances for the differences in population, national income, natural resources, and the comparative price index. France in that day had about one-sixth or one-seventh of the population of the United States of today, and her national income probably was proportionately less, because the chief enterprise was still a relatively primitive form of agriculture. Modestly estimated, a four-billion-livre debt weighed about as heavily on France in the 1780's as a debt of around twenty-five billion dollars would have weighed on the United States of the prewar period of the 1930's. Even in the present day of astronomical national debts, that is a staggering sum if allowance be made for the inflationary trends since the 1930's. The debt and the rising cost of living could not alone have brought on the French Revolution, but they were major contributing factors in the accumulating unrest. Both were in large measure directly attributable to French participation in the American Revolutionary War.

What is more important, general awareness that dissatisfaction was widespread throughout France, with a resultant solidarity among the dissatisfied, became much more marked after the 1770's. That too was attributable in large measure to French participation in the American Revolutionary War. To be sure, France was an absolute monarchy; the press was censored, and writers were sent to prison for the expression of heterodox opinions. The French had nevertheless been the allies of a confederation that believed in republican institutions. Several of those confederated states had constitutions containing bills of rights guaranteeing civil and political liberty. It became desirable for absolutist France to tolerate—in fact to build up—among its people a sympathy with the republican institutions of America, its ally.

It was now the patriotic duty not only of French writers to promote the interest of French people in the American nation but also of the censors not to interfere unnecessarily with their doing so. For example, in 1778 a collection was published of the constitutions of the states and the Declaration of Independence, which was dedicated to Benjamin Franklin and was referred to as "the code of liberty." In 1783 a much more impressive work reinforced the pro-American impact. It contained, besides the constitutions of the thirteen states, other significant American documents, although it was called *Les Constitutions des Treize États de l'Amérique.* It was of special significance that this work was published by the king's official printer. That meant, as was later pointed out when a French Revolutionary assembly issued the famous Declaration of the Rights of Man and of the Citizen, that a declaration of rights actually had been promulgated in France by royal consent several years earlier.

Another reason for the rapid spread of American ideals of liberty in France before the French Revolution was the personal popularity of Benjamin Franklin. He was petted by the ladies and feted by the aristocracy; he was lionized by the court and eulogized by poets, scientists and journalists; and he was envied by Arthur Lee and John Adams. The effect, direct or indirect, of Franklin's personal charm, his wide correspondence, and the writings about him was that the people of France often thought of all Americans as being made more or less in his image. The thought was probably far from true, but it did Americans no harm that their allies tended to think so.

Another channel for the favorable impact of American ideals upon French popular psychology was the impression made upon the soldiers who went from France to fight in the War of American Independence. Lafayette went back to France a worshipper of Washington and, for the most part, an uncritical admirer of American institutions. The Abbé Robin, who had been a chaplain with Rochambeau's army, wrote a book about his experience that spoke of the Americans as if they were a nation of new Arcadians. Chastellux, who already had a great reputation as a *philosophe* and was third in command to Rochambeau, wrote a volume on his journeys through America that induced its readers to believe that American institutions were ideal and the American people admirable. And a number of young men who, like Lafayette, were to become leaders in the forthcoming revolution in France—men like Alexandre de Lameth, Mathieu Dumas, the Comte de Ségur, the Vicomte de Noailles, and that Saint-Simon who became the founder of the famous school of socialist utopians in the nineteenth century—all stated in later years that they had imbibed their first ideas of liberty from their contact with Americans during the Revolutionary War. These people wrote, spoke, and made orations about the American people, American institutions, and American principles. They fondly nurtured idealizations of which they would brook no criticism. They flocked to the defense of the Americans whenever American virtues were questioned by others, like Deux Ponts, Moré, Biron, and Armand, who had hardly less right to speak of the American people than they. And the people of France, it proved, preferred to believe those who eulogized rather than those who disparaged America. The occasional book that criticized the United States won very little audience, whereas books like those of Chastellux and Robin received an enthusiastic welcome; and Lafayette became the most popular Frenchman of the day in France as well as America.

Another factor that led to the spread of American ideals in France was the active propaganda of French agents, both diplomatic and unofficial, in America. Crèvecoeur's famous *Letters from an American Farmer* spread broadcast a roseate picture of the United States in vastly different English and French editions. Foremost among the official propagandists was the Chevalier de La Luzerne, the French minister in Philadelphia. La Luzerne subsidized Americans, including Thomas Paine, to write things about America for circulation in France. Paine, according to La Luzerne, proved too lazy to write a reply to a critique of America by an illustrious *philosophe,* the Abbé Raynal, and La Luzerne satisfied himself by carefully going over the French translation of Carver's *Voyages through the Interior Parts of North America* and helping the translation to win approval in France.

So the king's government, on the one hand, promoted interest in American institutions, while, on the other, it opposed freedom in order to uphold absolute monarchy. This predicament arose largely because there was a war going on and France wanted to win it. Money had to be advanced and armies raised if it was to be won, and those things could not easily be done without popular support. The predicament was solved by weakening the royal censorship to the point where, in the famous "flood of pamphlets" of 1788, it practically collapsed.

Thus the 1770's marked a new era in the propagation of the ideas that formed the intellectual foundations of the French Revolution. The change was noticeable in two ways. In the first place, ideas of reform became common property, and no longer belonged exclusively to the literate classes. In the second place, they became concrete rather than abstract. The outstanding students of French public opinion during this period, like Daniel Mornet, find that before the 1770's the *philosophes* had appealed only to a limited audience, consisting almost exclusively of those who could afford to buy the very expensive books produced by the high publication costs of that day, and that they had dealt with mankind in broad general terms. But after the 1770's, as the appeal of the *philosophes* became more popular and was spread more widely than before—through conversations, law courts, sermons, masonic lodges, and club meetings, as well as books, it became more specific. The demand was now not alone for the general reform of mankind in accordance with "the laws of Nature and of Nature's God" but also for practical and immediate changes in French government and institutions. Even the authors of utopias tended to turn from picturing purely imaginary states to describing what an ideal France might someday be; and although none of them spelled *nature's* backward, one of them did spell *Paris* backward to make the name of his ideal city.

Madame d'Houdetot, a friend of Franklin, wrote to him that America had now provided the *philosophes* with "an example and a hope." In other words, America had become a case of Philosophy teaching by Example. In much the same way that speculative socialists of more recent times, unable to make a great impression upon the popular mind if they talked merely of what might be, found that, when they had an actual example in Russia, they could more easily bring about political pressure and effect political action, so the *philosophes,* the political theorists of the eighteenth century, once they could point to a living illustration of the Rights of Man in America, rallied behind them the type of person that could not grasp principles but could visualize the force of political reform in action. Old writers now began to write about American institutions rather than the abstract Rights of Man and the welfare of mankind in general. Condorcet, Raynal, Chastellux, Turgot and Mably were only a few of the figures among the recognized *philosophes* who turned their attention to America, writing critiques of the American constitutions and innovations. A set of new writers who would probably have developed into another generation of *philosophes* if their energies had not been diverted by the French Revolution also became leaders in the new American vogue. Men like Mirabeau and Brissot, not to mention Condorcet and Lafayette again, wrote about the new America, holding it up as an example of what a good state ought to be. France, they thought, could hardly become a republic; it was too big to be anything but a monarchy. Yet otherwise it might follow the American model profitably.

The attention these writers received was heightened by the controversies in which they engaged with Americans like Adams, Jefferson, Livingston, Mazzei and Barlow, and by translations of more sober historical and anthropological writings of American students like Filson, Carver and Ramsay. French journals carried articles on America —sometimes by Americans. Abbé Raynal's popular *History of the Two Indies* in the original edition of 1775 gave only twenty pages to the United States but in that of 1780 almost one hundred and fifty. Thus war, diplomacy and propaganda united to produce a general awareness of the existence of a restless spirit in France.

France had, however, long been restless. Nearly every decade since Louis XIV's death had witnessed a revolutionary crisis. But the repeated crises that had flared up to the danger point had in the end died down without producing catastrophe. One reason for the ineffectiveness of these outbursts was that they had had no enterprising leadership. The American Revolution now helped to supply that deficiency. An actual, though far from exhaustive, count has been made of Frenchmen who took a leading part in both the American and the French Revolution. There were thirty-eight of them, including Lafayette, the Lameth brothers, the Rochambeaus (father and son), Duportail, Estaing, Dumas, Ségur, Jourdan, Gouvion, Noailles, Custine, Beauharnais, Montmorency-Laval—to mention only those who were conspicuously friendly to the French Revolution in its initial stages. Of these, as we have noted, several admitted that they owed much of their interest in revolutionary ideas to America. How far the American Revolution was a factor in training men, like Brissot, Condorcet, Dupont, Marat and Robespierre, who were not soldiers, for their roles in the French Revolution can be only a matter of conjecture. It would be rash to believe that such men, but for the American development, would not have become revolutionary leaders. Yet they followed American affairs and watched the republican experiment with keen interest, as their writings and speeches make abundantly clear.

Thus the American Revolution helped to provide leaders for the French Revolution and made it possible for unrest to result in more effective demands for reform. It did more than that, however. It also furnished a model, a program, and a political philosophy for those leaders. As we have already seen, the French philosophers no longer had to talk about abstractions like natural law, natural institutions and natural morality derived from a hypothetical Common Sense or Reason. They no longer had to seek in the wilds of America or Asia for the theoretical Child of Nature. In live Americans like Benjamin Franklin they now found an impressive exemplar of a people who had actually achieved a life and a society that a philosopher might embrace. Across the Atlantic, as anyone who was not willfully blind could see, vigorous states prospered with governments based upon the Rights of Man.

To be sure, the *philosophes* deceived themselves somewhat. Franklin fell a little short of being a paragon, and the United States of being Arcadia. Yet it was more convincing to cite concrete cases than to point to sublimated primitives or to hypothetical societies. The American Arcadia, if not examined too critically, fully justified the speculations of the philosopher, Why could not Arcadia be located also in France?

With such queries political propaganda in France took on a more specific, pragmatic and effective form. The illiterate on the café terrace of the smallest village could grasp what the new generation of *philosophes* was saying as readily as the learned in the salons of the capital. Lafayette was not alone in noting that liberal ideas spread rapidly throughout France after the American Revolution. Talleyrand remarked that subsequent to the victory over England America became "the sole topic of conversation" among the aristocracy; and the English agriculturalist Arthur Young observed in his travels in France in 1787 "a strong leaven of liberty, increasing every hour since the American revolution."

No man's testimony in this regard can be more convincing than Thomas Jefferson's. As American minister to France, he was sympathetic with the reform party, particularly with Lafayette, who had no secrets from him, and he knew more about the American Revolution than any other man in France. When the French Revolution was unmistakably on its way, he wrote the well-known English liberal Dr. Richard Price his interpretation of how it had come about: "Though celebrated writers of this and other countries had already sketched good principles on the subject of government, yet the American war seems first to have awakened the thinking part of this nation in general from the sleep of despotism in which they were sunk. The officers too who had been to America were mostly young men, less shackled by habit and prejudice, and more ready to assent to the dictates of common sense and common right. They came back impressed with these. The press, notwithstanding its shackles, began to disseminate them; conversation, too, assumed new freedom; politics became the theme of all societies, male and female, and a very extensive and zealous party was formed, which may be called the Patriotic party, who, sensible of the abusive government under which they lived, longed for occasions of reforming it."

Yet, if my theory of the causes of revolution is right, provocations, crystallized public opinion, popular leaders, and a program of reform, even when they occur together, do not make a revolution unless the conservative forces are too weak to resist change effectively. Here, too, the American contribution was significant. The royal debt, by weakening the French treasury, made revision of the fiscal system inescapable. Furthermore, although there was still very little republicanism in France after the American Revolution, many more among the influential circles than before favored thoroughgoing reform of the monarchy. Important, too, in creating weakness of the conservative forces was the fact that aristocratic officers who had returned from the war in America could no longer be counted upon to obey if ordered to shoot down opponents of the government. An "American faction" also grew up in the parlements, and a "liberal aristocracy" at court, with Lafayette foremost among them. The same conditions that provided leaders for the revolutionaries created disaffection among the conservatives at the very time when the conservatives should have presented a united front if the Old Régime were to be preserved.

It goes without saying that the conditions which together made reformers willing to risk revolution and conservatives unable to resist it—a combination which makes revolution inevitable—naturally did not come exclusively from the American shore. The American Revolution had less effect on the French peasants, who formed about three-fourths of France's population, or on the city workers, or on the lower clergy than on the upper classes, except as its influence seeped down from the aristocracy and the middle class or as it was reflected in general agitation, fiscal difficulties and the rising cost of living. But upon the aristocracy and the middle class that influence was great. And the French Revolution at the outset was a movement of the aristocracy and the middle class.

On the eve of the French upheaval, Baron Friedrich Melchior de Grimm, though himself a friend of the *philosophes*, intimated that Frenchmen might well regret America if they stopped to think. "Her liberty has cost France nearly two billions," he wrote. ". . . That costly glory will serve only to hasten a revolution the outbreak of which all the nations of Southern Europe would seem well advised at least to put off, if the force of circumstances should make it inevitable." Louis XVI himself recognized that the American Revolution was the source of his troubles. The French Revolution had just begun when Sultan Tippoo of Mysore asked for French aid in driving the English out of India. Louis XVI, hesitating to comply, commented dryly: "This occasion greatly resembles the American affair, of which I never think without regret. On that occasion they took advantage somewhat of my youth, and today we are paying the penalty for it. The lesson is too vivid to be forgotten."

It is now about half a century since Lord Acton gave his deservedly famous lectures on the French Revolution at Cambridge University. I can find no better words to end my argument than those he used to begin his lecture on "The Influence of America":

> The several structures of political thought that arose in France, and clashed in the process of revolution, were not directly responsible for the outbreak. The doctrines hung like a cloud upon the heights, and at critical moments in the reign of Louis XV men felt that a catastrophe was impending. It befell when there was less provocation, under his successor; and the spark that changed thought into action was supplied by the Declaration of American Independence. It was the system of an international extra-territorial universal Whig, far transcending the English model by its simplicity and rigour. It surpassed in force all the speculation of Paris and Geneva, for it had undergone the test of experiment and its triumph was the most memorable thing that had been seen by men.

The Declaration of the Rights of Man and of the Citizen and Mr. Jellinek

EMILE BOUTMY

Emile Gaston Boutmy (1835–1906) began his career as journalist and lecturer in the history of civilization and comparative architecture at the *Ecole spéciale d'architecture* in Paris. In founding the *Ecole libre des sciences politiques* in 1872, Boutmy became the godfather of French political science, which became a recognized discipline largely under his inspiration. His own writings included studies on the political psychology of both the English and the American peoples.

A HIGHLY respected professor of the University of Heidelberg, Mr. Jellinek, has created some interest in Germany by recently publishing a work on the Declaration of Rights which introduces our constitution of 1791. . . . [Mr. Jellinek's thesis] may be summarized as follows: The Declaration of Rights did not, as had been widely held, stem from the Social Contract but is its very antithesis. As can be demonstrated by the most cursory textual comparison, the origins and models of the Declaration may be found in the Bills of Rights at the head of the constitutions of the American states which went into effect between 1776 and 1789.

Religious freedom is the oldest element among these declarations. The Anglo-Saxon colonies of the New World pioneered in recognizing and subscribing to it. . . . Hence there gradually emerged the concept of recognizing and adopting other liberties in a similar way. This explains why the earliest documents purporting to present a list of the rights of man and the citizen originated in America. All of the declarations of rights thus have their source in evangelical liberty, and the most famous of all of them—that of 1789—is tied to the Reformation of the sixteenth century by definite and authenticated links, however difficult they may be to trace.

I will not stoop to consider whether Mr. Jellinek unconsciously gave way to a very natural inclination in finding a Germanic source for the most striking demonstration of the Latin spirit at the end of the eighteenth century. . . . The only validity which I can see in his conclusion is that the example of America and its Declaration of Independence (rather than the little-known constitutions of its states) may have contributed to the idea of combining under a single heading the rights of man and of the citizen as a preamble to the Constitution. . . . None of Mr. Jellinek's other assertions can, in my view, be reconciled with the kind of balanced view of the facts and documents in which I could wholly concur: all of them seem equally dubious to me. . . .

Mr. Jellinek, convinced of the influence

From Emile Boutmy, "La Déclaration des Droits de l'Homme et du Citoyen et M. Jellinek," *Annales des Sciences politiques,* XVII (1902), 415–443. Translated by the Editor.

of the United States of America, was thereby bound to discount Rousseau's impact. He dismisses quite judiciously, as I have done, the hypothesis that our constitutionalists might have modeled themselves either on the Declaration of Independence of 1776 or on the amendments to the Constitution. Yet with a conviction seemingly backed by documentary evidence, he cites the Bills of Rights of the individual states promulgated between 1776 and 1789 as the main source upon which the authors of our Declaration drew. This deserves examination and gives rise to some reflection.

Before seeking direct textual proof of the resemblances between the Declaration of Rights and the constitutions of individual American states, Mr. Jellinek refers to some circumstantial evidence. Let me show by example what he has in mind. In the course of the debates which began on July 11, 1789, Lafayette was the first orator who spoke of the necessity for a declaration and sought to provide a model. Under these circumstances one could expect him to make a clear-cut allusion to the American Bill of Rights, which he would certainly have been able to recall. Yet no such allusion was made; hence Mr. Jellinek is obliged to look for his evidence in a much later document, the *Memoirs* of Lafayette in which the Bills of Rights are mentioned as furnishing a basis for his argument. In point of fact, while it is highly significant that Lafayette should have ignored the American Bills of Rights in introducing his declaration, it is not at all remarkable that years later he should have related and even ascribed this declaration to the precedent of the Virginia constitution. Such an association of ideas was clearly hindsight and retained because it made sense and served to lend unity to Lafayette's career. . . .

The circumstantial evidence has neither convinced nor even disturbed us. Is the direct evidence more persuasive? Mr. Jellinek in his Chapter V simply provides the text of the French and American documents without comment, counting on the common sense and good faith of the reader to perceive the close resemblance and hence the relationship between the two documents.

Before undertaking this sort of confrontation, several remarks are called for. First of all, rather than a single American text, there are seven or eight. From among these documents, Mr. Jellinek has naturally singled out those articles which show the closest relationship to the French Declaration, while equally naturally neglecting those which do not fit. . . . The procedure used by Mr. Jellinek is therefore somewhat suspect, as it gives rise to serious error: quite possibly he might convey the impression that half of the French articles are borrowed from American texts, whereas a more accurate comparison of each of the constitutions in their entirety might, for instance, reduce the percentage of analogies to five or ten per cent.

I submit a second observation to the good sense and fair-mindedness of the reader. Mr. Jellinek is not unaware that among the sources for the American Declarations is English Common Law, to which should be added Magna Carta, the Petition of Rights, the Act of Settlement. Since the Common Law is for the most part unwritten, this cannot be cited. Yet he footnotes several references to Magna Carta and succeeding documents, citing the case of every man's right to be judged by his peers and the principle that no man may be taxed without his own consent or that of his representatives. I find it difficult to believe that these and other principles, recognized and practiced for centuries in England, should have had to cross the breadth of the Atlantic before coming back to us. It is more likely that they may have made a direct Channel crossing to exert some influence either on the Declaration of Rights as such or on the common fund of eighteenth century ideas from which this declaration drew. This would mean discounting the impact of the American Bills of Rights on our Constitution of 1789.

Another objection which Mr. Jellinek

can scarcely avoid is the reminder that a common ideology of the eighteenth century based on Locke, Montesquieu, Voltaire, Rousseau, prevailed throughout the civilized world, including the American colonies. The speculative concepts of the Declaration of Rights drew upon this ideological reservoir. Rousseau's ideas, if not his books, had made their impact on men's minds, however forgotten their originator and however anonymous the garb which they assumed. Besides, one of the characteristics of the period was the use of abstract maxims as the fountainhead from which everything else flowed. These maxims were in a sense the uniform worn by the eighteenth century. The rule, or at least the fashion, of the times called for a mode of thought and expression couched in general terms.

Toward 1760 France, Holland, England and the United States shared this manner of reasoning and a particular way of arguing which was not peculiar to any one of them. These countries elaborated upon ideas drawn from this common treasury at their leisure and according to their particular genius. Thus the similarities that may be observed between certain American declarations and the French Declaration should not lead us to infer direct influence, but rather the influence of a common model. . . . No borrowing of one document from the other may be detected.

An absolute distinction must, however, be drawn between the American Bills of Rights and our Declaration in another respect, namely their difference in aim, in the ultimate objective of their being drawn up and promulgated. All of the American Declarations were worded in such a way that they could be invoked before . . . the Supreme Court of their state, and they therefore listed juridical arguments of relevance to judicial proceedings: the American Declarations' context reflects this preoccupation. For the French, the Declaration was a piece of oratory whose articles had no teeth, no more force than the majestic sway which truth held over all men. No court could accept any of its articles as source of precedent for a judgment. The French wrote to enlighten the world, while the American constitutionalists composed the articles of their Declaration for the advantage and convenience of their fellow citizens; hence a notable difference in tone and intention as between the two types of documents. . . . The French Declaration of Rights is written in the spare and daring style of a *philosophe* concerned only with expressing a universal truth. The American Declarations of Rights, on the other hand, reflect the somewhat meticulous and dense language of the legal expert anxious to include any means that might help a litigant. . . . The one document is all nobility of structure, grandeur of form, while the other deals in terms of a propriety, accuracy and comprehensiveness which will enhance the practical ends for which the document may serve. No two documents in this world are more dissimilar.

. . . I shall deal one by one with the articles of the French Declaration and compare them to the relevant sections of the American Declarations. It will be surprising, I believe, to show what such a careful examination demonstrates.

Article 1:

> Men are born, and always continue free and equal with respect to their rights. Civil distinctions, therefore, can be founded only on public utility.

In this first article a contrast stands out: Frenchmen are born and remain free and equal in rights, with equality put on the same level as liberty. Furthermore, rather than any equality of status, that is, of intelligence and wealth which would run counter to common sense, only equality before the law is proclaimed. What does the American Declaration claim? That men are "by nature equally free and independent." Equality is confined to an adverb, in a way hiding behind the two adjectives which express the basic idea. While America is not indifferent to equality, the latter is such a routine by-product of the basic conditions of American society that it was not worth making a separate point of it. . . .

Article 2 mentions the preservation of the inalienable rights of man as the final aim of political association: namely, liberty, property, security and resistance to oppression. All these rights are also cited in the American Declarations even though never in this all-inclusive form, yet the tone is very different from the French Declaration. The style of the French document—terse, clear, dry, imperious—contrasts with the style of the American documents, the involutions of which betray the hand of the lawyer. . . .

The third article shows us clearly the contrast between *philosophe* and legal expert. In the American text the word "power" which expresses something concrete and tangible takes the place of "sovreignty," a term which is essentially metaphysical. The phrase, "habitually belongs to the nation," is part of everyday language, while by contrast "is vested in the people" leads us into the midst of legal terminology. As to the second part of the phrase in the French Declaration, "Nor can any individual, or any body of men, be entitled to any authority which is not expressly derived from it," it has no American equivalent for reasons that are obvious. A nation which still retained or had just abolished estates such as the nobility and the clergy, corporate bodies such as the sovereign courts, was naturally anxious to block their return to power. Nothing analogous prevailed in the United States and hence the Americans could dispense with the anxiety and the precaution. . . .

Article 6 is conceived as follows:

Law is the expression of the general will. All citizens have the right to participate directly or through their representatives in its formulation. It should be the same for all, whether it protects or punishes, and all citizens being equal in its sight, are equally eligible to all honors, places, and employments according to their different abilities, without any other distinction than that created by their virtues and talents.

This passage contains four ideas only one of which appears in the American texts, namely the concept which in all Anglo-Saxon lands has been the basis of a representative government. The documents cited by Mr. Jellinek repeat one after the other that laws are only valid insofar as they have been drawn up by the citizens or their representatives. One of them, moreover, adds in imitation of the Bill of Rights that elections must be free. Another one mentions the qualifications needed for the franchise. Nowhere do the three remaining ideas appear among these supposed models of the French Declaration: the idea that law must be the expression of the general will, that it must be equal for everyone, that all citizens are eligible for all offices. . . .

I have no intention to continue this comparative analysis, which is tedious since it can only reinforce a conclusion already reached. Having said enough to indicate clearly the features which distinguish the two declarations and which remove any suspicions that they might indeed be related, I shall confine myself to listing for the remaining articles those parts of the French Declaration which do not have any counterparts in the American documents.

In Article 9 the French lawmaker declares that anyone exercising public power who used unjustifiable harshness in carrying out the arrest of a person must be punished. Nothing similar can be found in the American Declarations.

In Article 10 one may observe completely contrasting views on religion:

It is the right as well as the duty of all men in society, publicly, and at stated seasons, to worship the Supreme Being, the great Creator and Preserver of the universe. And no subject shall be hurt, molested or restrained, in his person, liberty, or estate, for worshipping God in the manner and season most agreeable to the dictates of his own conscience; or for his religious profession of sentiments; provided he doth not disturb the public peace or obstruct others in their religious worship. . . .

The French text is peculiarly brief: it maintains freedom of opinions and in addition freedom "even of religious opinions." Elaboration and long-windedness, on the other hand, characterize the American documents:

Every man is guaranteed the natural and inalienable right to worship God according to the command of his conscience and his reason. No one may be attacked, injured, molested or impeded in his person, liberty or property for having worshipped God in the manner and at the time which are in harmony with the commands of his own conscience, or declared faith, sentiments or convictions, provided he does not disturb public peace or injure other citizens in the exercise of their religion.

In this instance . . . one has the feeling that Americans are incapable of a philosophy which goes beyond religious apologia; they are intent on establishing the validity of Christianity in the manner of Channing as a sort of natural religion. French philosophy of the period claimed to transcend all kinds of religious belief. . . .

In Article 12 there is a complete divergence. While the American Declaration repeats the banal truth borrowed from the Declaration of Independence that all governments are instituted for the common welfare and the protection of their citizens, the French legislator deals with the make-up of armed forces—army constabulary, police—institutions which are essential to the guarantee of rights to the citizen and which are never to be employed for private ends by those holding authority.

Articles 13 and 14 spell out with great precision everything concerning taxes. They mention, for example, the fact that taxes should be proportionate to the taxpayer's ability to pay, that all citizens, personally or by delegation, should ascertain the need for taxes, consent to them freely, verify their expenditure and determine their allocation, basis, collection and duration.

Almost none of these essential specific points are mentioned in the American text which is confined to listing that each citizen owed his share of the taxes and that no subsidy be established and levied on the taxpayer without the consent of the people or its representatives. Those are the very terms of the Petition of Rights to which, in the course of a century, nothing had been added. What a contrast to the French Declaration which ignores none of the conditions which make for a healthy political economy in the area of taxation.

The first of the last three articles is about the only one which bears out Mr. Jellinek's observations. In dealing with the responsibilities of officials, both documents are identical in content and form. Article 17 where expropriation for reasons of public welfare is mentioned also conforms exactly to the American article, yet in this instance we are a long way from the great maxims to which the Declaration of Rights has accustomed us. Only the sixteenth article has some significance and some bearing. In this article, coming at the very end of the Declaration at a time when evidently there was not much more to be said, one finds that most important axiom of political science, the separation of powers. Never has a document been clearer in demonstrating that the French had little interest in advocating, still less in practicing, Montesquieu's maxim. In contrast this maxim did leave a deep imprint on men's minds in America and it is not astonishing to note that the constitutions of the individual states should have made a point of spelling out with clarity and complacency what, a few years later, was to become the foundation of the Federal Constitution. Here is another last and striking example of the almost constant contradiction between the French and the American documents. . . .

It remains for us to disentangle the origins . . . of political and civil liberties. These liberties fall into two categories: there are those which result from any civilized state, from the legal suppression of artificial and traditional inequalities—equality before the law and the courts, equality of taxation, equal eligibility to offices and finally, the right which guarantees all others, equality at the ballot box. It may be said that these are not really liberties, yet no one will call a people free who is deprived of them. In fact, the colonists possessed the first three freedoms, equality before the law, of taxation and equal eligibility to office. Such freedoms went into effect when Americans had set up an organized society, hence there was no need for a precedent-shattering law to lend them authority and prestige. This type of freedom had originated "in the nature of things" and in the circumstances of the first social contract. The last freedom, that of suffrage, was for understandable reasons somewhat delayed compared to the others. All of the liberties, however, encountered exceptionally favorable circumstances. Imagine a group of immigrants arriving in Massachusetts in the north of what is today the United States. These men, who knew each other, shared the same religion, faced a common inescapable problem, namely that of providing a civil and political organization for themselves. While they brought their allegiance to the English king, this king had only a nominal authority, and hence they could only find the effective authority which they required in the community itself meeting as a group. The majority within this meeting would decide what rules had to be made, creating judicial offices and appointing the magistrates. As governor, treasurer, judges, administrative officers were needed, all or most of these offices were named by town meeting which would also formulate and promulgate laws as they became necessary. . . .

Democracy in its most extreme form was indispensable to these people. They were not burdened by any of the traditional privileges which prevailed in their home countries. They were "reborn," as their Bible claimed, once they had reached this land which was almost deserted and had no history; hence the society which they organized had nothing in common with that of old Europe.

Granted that the case of New England is extreme. Let us therefore turn to the immigrants of other colonies, particularly Virginia where a part of the English gentry had settled. On its great plantations (the equivalent of the British latifundia) among its Negroes and poor whites, this gentry pursued the life of rather coarse and uneducated squires. Apparently elements of a new nobility, a nobility of privilege could be found there. Yet on whom could these planters have leaned for support, to what authority could they have appealed to confirm their privileges in the face of the expanding population which surrounded them? In Europe the noble owed his exceptional situation, ratified by law, to one of two ancient facts: conquest and the hierarchical organization of landed property. In America conquest, to the extent that there ever was such a parallel, was over once the mass of colonists had prevailed over the scattered Indian tribal groups. . . . On an almost virgin continent, a thousand miles wide, land could not become a monopoly and the power basis on which privilege could be founded. In Europe the nobility, entrenched in its hereditary privileges by a sympathetic royalty, proved at all times the great obstacle to the establishment of the egalitarian liberties which have been mentioned. In America, however, there were no hereditary immunities nor a monarchy capable of guaranteeing them. . . .

In summary, liberties were born naturally on American soil. These liberties only required religious freedom as their prototype. Each freedom enjoyed as much prestige as any other. These liberties evolved to the point where they could be gathered in Bills of Rights which Americans, prompted by the very spirit of the eighteenth century, were to use as preambles to their constitutions.

A second type of liberty remains to be

considered: the right of assembly and of association, freedom of the press, judicial liberties and finally, religious freedom. The hallmark of these liberties is that they may be granted without prejudice to any class of citizens in preference to any other. They concern the state alone, threaten only the state, and imply a partial surrender of state power. . . . Hence they largely depend on the particular nature of the state. Wherever the notion of the state has a purely historical or even mystical basis which is indefensible in the face of criticism . . . the government will be reluctant to grant extensive rights. . . . Where, on the contrary, historical or mystical elements have been jettisoned in favor of purely rational elements, such as in the case of a republic, fewer obstacles to the discussion of the fundamental principles of government will be encountered. A republican constitution relying on reason as its creative and organizing essence . . . can afford to grant such powerful means of action which had helped to create the republic. Yet freedom of assembly, of association and of the press are a dangerous threat to authority which has an indefinite term of office. By contrast these liberties are essential where authority is limited by a definite term. The victorious party is careful not to tamper with the perquisites which made its victory possible, while the ousted party sees in it its chances for the next election. America offers a striking example of this law. . . .

How far we have come from the Reformation, or from the liberty of conscience which furnished a model and framework for other freedoms! Of these liberties, some were but the necessary consequence of a specific social organization which was naturally exempt from all privilege, indeed from all inequality; others owed their existence to the very nature of a republican state. . . . [As to the French Declaration] I believe that the whole eighteenth century, destructive of all tradition and creating natural right, must be credited with the sensible and vigorous conclusions of the Declaration of the Rights of Man and of the Citizen. . . .

The Myth of the French Revolution

ALFRED COBBAN

HISTORY, said Napoleon, is a myth that men agree to believe. I would rather say that it is this so long as it is something which it is important to them to believe or not. While the past lives it remains a myth, and naturally like all things living, it changes. The history of the French Revolution, whether garbed in the apocalyptic vision of a Carlyle or the profound scholarship of a Lefebvre, has continued to live and to change because it has continued to be bound up with the beliefs and aspirations of mankind.

I am tempted to suggest that in another sense also the French Revolution might be called a myth. At first, I must confess, I thought of entitling this lecture, "Was there a French Revolution?" However, it seemed that to inaugurate this chair by eliminating the Revolution would be rather awkward; and it would certainly have been tactless to invite our French friends here and begin by abolishing their Revolution for them. I am therefore asking a safer question: "What was the French Revolution?" We used to think that it began in 1789. Now we know it began at least in 1787. It ended when? In 1815? Thiers and Aulard conclude their histories of the Revolution in 1799, Mathiez and Thompson in 1794, Guérin begins the reaction in 1793, Salvemini ends his history in 1792, and for some it has never ended. To each terminal date corresponds a different interpretation. Worse still follows. The Revolution has ceased to be a revolution and become a series of revolutions—the last Fronde of the nobles and the *parlements:* the revolution of the *tiers état,* the peasant rising, the republican insurrection, the revolt of the *sans-culottes,* the *neuf thermidor* and the various *coups d'état* under the Directory ending in that of *18 brumaire.* The French Revolution is in fact a name we give to a long series of events. What it means depends on the light in which we see the connection between these events. In this sense the French Revolution, if not a myth, is a theory, or rather a number of rival theories. . . .

. . . In a single separate event what we call chance or accident may be admitted; a universal, world-shaking movement such as the French Revolution seems to force determinism upon us. Historians of the Revolution, particularly of recent times, have increasingly tended to show why all that happened *had* to happen. The historian may not be able to see the strings which move his figures. It may be more interesting for him to pretend to forget them and describe his puppet play as though the actors moved of their own volition. But the really serious historian likes to think that this is make-believe, and prefers to concentrate on the mechanics of the process rather than on the mere twitches of arms and legs which stimulate free action. But why should he stop at this? If there is one level of truth in the description of the movements of the puppets, and another in tracing the strings, the real historical causation, it is sometimes

From Alfred Cobban, *The Myth of the French Revolution: an Inaugural Lecture* (London, 1955). Reprinted by permission of the author.

held, is to be found in the hidden forces that control them both. These are not to be seen but they may be deduced, as the Greeks detected the vagaries of the inhabitants of Olympus behind the changing destinies of their clients and victims here below. Of course, the new Olympus is infinitely more respectable. The wanton favours and enmities of a pack of uninhibited gods and goddesses no longer bring superhuman success or inhuman punishment. Great impersonal forces have taken their place, or rather a single great impersonal force, which is there operating unseen all the time, though only when there is a great revolution in human destinies, we are told, do we become fully aware of its ceaseless inexorable working, before which one social order passes away and in the predetermined pattern of history, another emerges.

To pass from the general to the particular, in the French Revolution, it is commonly said, the feudal order passed away and the rule of the bourgeoisie took its place. This is, put simply, the myth which has dominated serious research on the history of the French Revolution during the present century. It is often treated as an exemplification of a scientific law derived from the facts of history. If I am calling it a myth, this is in no derogatory sense but in a Platonic way of speaking, which may, of course, be worse. The fact that it has come to be taken for granted is my reason for re-examining it. Simplifying, but then this is essentially a *conte de fées,* the outline of the story is that there was once a social order called feudalism. This was a terrible ogre and lived in a castle; but for centuries a bourgeois Jack the Giant-killer climbed the beanstalk of economic progress, until finally in the French Revolution he liquidated the old order and put in its place something called alternatively bourgeois society or capitalism. The only divergence from the traditional story is that he did not live happily ever after. I think it would be fair to say that this is the generally accepted myth or theory of the French Revolution, and of course both the factors in it are themselves theories. I propose to discuss them in turn.

The first is feudalism. This is a term that was invented to describe the social organization that prevailed in the Middle Ages. By the time of the French Revolution, as a system of government based on the ownership of land it had long come to an end in France. Not only had the feudal aristocracy ceased to govern the country, it had even ceased to own a large part of the land. A rough estimate is that one-third of the land had passed into the possession of the peasantry, and a fair proportion of the remainder was forest or waste. The so-called feudalism of the eighteenth century consisted in the survival of antiquated dues and services owed to the descendants of the former feudal seigneurs, or to those who had purchased their *seigneuries.* A considerable body of *feudistes* lived out of the continual law-suits that these claims, registered in *terriers,* involved. In the years before 1789 an attempt was made by the possessors of feudal rights—and possibly in particular by their new possessors, though this is a matter that requires investigation—to revive old ones that had long fallen into disuse and to enforce surviving ones more rigorously. In spite of this, they remained a peculiarly functionless survival, the relics of an atrophied organ, which only a very adventurous social biologist could use to justify a classification with some fossil feudal order of the past. In the words of a legal historian, the fief, in the eighteenth century, was *une forme bizarre de propriété foncière.* The jurists of the time admitted that the *"seigneur utile,"* that is to say the *tenancier,* was the real proprietor, though his property involved certain obligations, which they described in legal terminology as a *"servitude au profit du seigneur foncier."*

How little the so-called feudal dues deserved their title was to be proved in the course of the attempt to apply the decrees of 4–11 August 1789, by which the Constituent Assembly proposed to abolish those dues that were feudal in origin, while at the same time maintaining those payments of services which were of the nature of economic rent. It proved impossible to make the distinction in practice and after years of legal struggle the attempt was abandoned and all dues which qualified ownership disappeared. This was just what the Constituent Assembly had feared and tried to avoid, for to suggest that the members of the Assembly wanted to abolish dues which many of them had acquired themselves would be a mistake. On the contrary, their disappearance was an unlooked-for and unwanted by-product of the Revolution. The night of the Fourth of August was not quite the spontaneous and generous gesture it has been made to seem. The men of property who sat in the Constituent Assembly, as Professor Lefebvre has pointed out, could not approve of confiscatory methods of dealing with property, especially when some of it was their own. The countryside took matters into its own hands when it broke out in the last *jacquerie,* under the stimulus of economic distress, the excitement of the drawing up of the *cahiers* and the election of the *tiers état,* and the general breakdown of authority resulting from the *révolte nobiliaire*. The unrest in the spring and summer of 1789 was so widespread that a major military operation would have been necessary to suppress it. The night of the Fourth of August was an attempt by throwing overboard some of the dues to salvage the rest. In the age of Reason, feudal went with such terms of abuse as Gothic and medieval. If the property rights that were sacrificed were called feudal, this was at least in part to prevent the episode from becoming a precedent in respect of other property rights. It was necessary to give the dog a bad name in order to justify his having been hanged. But the peasantry did not draw such subtle legal distinctions. They simply ceased to pay their dues, whatever their nature, and no subsequent government had the strength to make them resume payment. In the words of Lefebvre, "they liberated themselves, and the successive Assemblies only sanctioned what they had accomplished." If the system of seigneurial rights can be identified with the medieval social order called feudal; and if the reluctant acceptance of a *fait accompli* by the Constituent Assembly can be called abolishing feudalism, then, I suppose, the first part of the prevailing myth of the Revolution can hold good. The qualifications seem to me so extensive as to make the statement practically meaningless.

What of the other factor in the theory, the revolt of the bourgeoisie? It is unnecessary nowadays to labour the point that the Revolution began as an aristocratic rising; the Counterrevolution, as it subsequently became, in fact preceded the Revolution by at least two years. It has been described as the last Fronde and it marked the ultimate failure of Louis XIV's effort to place the monarchy so far above the privileged classes that they could never again challenge its authority as they had done during his minority. Of set purpose he had excluded the old *noblesse* from positions of authority in the state. Under the *grand monarque* the son of a linen-draper of Rouen, Colbert, could become the greatest man in the realm after the king, while only one man of noble birth was allowed in a ministerial office. Under his weaker successors the Court took its revenge and nobles infiltrated into the government of the state. They monopolized the higher ranks of the Church and the Army, filled the *Conseil d'en haut* and supplied occupants for nearly all the ministries except that of the Controller General. The calling of the Assembly of Notables was a tacit recognition that the King could not govern against the will of the privileged orders, but instead of gaining their support he found that by giving them an organ of self expression he had merely opened the flood-gates of aristocratic revolt.

The last of the Frondes was in appearance a formidable movement. In reality it was an attempt by a class of parasites to take over the body politic, which they possessed the power to destroy but not to recreate. It was a revolt of the drones, for though nobles might occupy places of influence and power, the one thing the *noblesse* as a class did not do was work. There were, of course, exceptions, but, by and large, the *noblesse de race* had no field of active service to the state except the army, in which its numbers and courage did not make up for its indiscipline and inefficiency. French society had become etiolated, and if it could still produce fine flowers at the top, it was at the expense of the health of the whole plant. Nobles occupied positions of dignity and remuneration, the Court *noblesse* relied for its finances increasingly on the profits of places and pensions, but nearly all the effective business of the state was done by men a grade lower down. In the embassies one finds that *chargés* or secretaries, emerging from lower social strata, often performed most of the real work of diplomacy. In the *généralités* the duties of the *intendants*—now almost invariably noble even if their nobility was sometimes of rather recent vintage—were increasingly falling into the hands of the *secrétaire de l'intendance* and the *subdélégués,* as was shown by the fact that *intendants* themselves sometimes stayed away from their *généralités* for long periods. The ministries in Paris were dependent on the work of their permanent officials. The efficient officers in the army were largely those whose social origins prevented them from rising to the higher ranks. The legal work of France was carried out not by some thousand proud *parlementaires* but by a host of minor judicial officers. From commerce the *noblesse* was generally excluded under penalty of *dérogeance;* and though it was easy for wealthy *roturiers* to pass into the ranks of the *noblesse,* they could only do so by abandoning their effective functions and *vivant noblement.* Some nobles, or at least *ennoblés,* might be found as exceptions to these statements, but as a broad generalization it may be said that it was all those who did the real work of administering France who formed the *tiers état.* These men were drawn from and constituted an important, perhaps even the greatest, element in the bourgeoisie: and this brings me to the second of my problems, for bourgeois is a term used almost as loosely as feudalism.

In Great Britain we commonly think of the rise of the bourgeoisie as the rise of that class which was primarily concerned with the control of trade, industry and finance, as composed therefore of merchants, bankers, industrialists and capitalists, great and small. The accepted theory of the French Revolution is that it came when the new form of property which such men represented replaced the older form represented by the feudal landowners. Is this a correct analysis? I must begin by premising that if it was a revolt of the "monied men," to use Burke's term, it was certainly not provoked by economic grievances. The fine eighteenth-century quarters of French provincial towns are standing evidence of the wealth of the men who built them, as well as of the standards of taste that dictated their elegance. However, it is hardly necessary to discuss the reasons they might, or might not, have had for making a revolution until we are quite sure that they made it. Now, in fact, the men who made the Revolution of 1789 were the members of the Constituent Assembly; little of what had been achieved by 1791 was to be lost, and most of what was done subsequently was to be undone. The essential first question to ask, then, is who formed the *tiers état* of 1789?

Were they the representatives of a rising industrial capitalist class? To imagine that this was even possible would be to antedate such industrial revolution as France was to experience by more than half a century. Some kind of clue to their importance in society will be provided if we ask how many manufacturers there were among those elected in 1789. Those who actually sat in the Assembly, either as deputies or *suppléants*, in the *tiers état*, numbered 648. Among these there were just eight who are described as manufacturers or *maîtres de forges*. Perhaps, however, the bourgeois were the merchants? Some 76 of the *tiers* are described as *marchands* or *négociants*. Only about 20 of these came from places of any commercial importance; the remainder should perhaps be regarded primarily as local notables. Very few of them seem to have played any prominent part in the Revolution. The world of finance produced one solitary banker, though one merchant also described himself as a banker. Together, merchants, manufacturers and financiers amount to 85, or 13 per cent of the whole number.

If they were not merchants or manufacturers, then, what were the *tiers état* of 1789? The category of those concerned with trade and industry is easy to identify. The social status or function of the others is apt to be more difficult to distinguish, sometimes for lack of sufficient indication —*"bourgeois vivant noblement"* is fairly easy to place, as is even *"citoyen"*; but what is the significance of *"bourgeois fils aîné"*? Sometimes there appears also that great handicap which the modern historian suffers from as compared with the historian of medieval or ancient times, too much information. How is one to classify a member (of the Convention) described as "landowner, leather manufacturer, lawyer and professor of mathematics and physics?" My figures are, therefore, all approximate, but I do not think that a variation of a few either way would do much to alter the general picture that emerges of the kind of men who composed the *tiers état* of 1789.

It is usually said that the majority were lawyers. This is undoubtedly true, but it is not as illuminating a statement as might be supposed. True, we can make out an impressive list of well over 400 lawyers in the Constituent Assembly, but this description tells us little about their actual social status or functions. It is as useful as would be a contemporary social classification based on the possession of a university degree.

Fortunately we know something more about most of the members. Those who are described as lawyers (*avocats* or *notaires*) without any further qualification number 166, just about a quarter, and it might be held that this was quite enough for the health of the Assembly. The remainder of the huge legal contingent falls into a different category. It includes members of the *ministère public,* notaries royal, local judges, municipal officers, and above all *lieutenants généraux* of *bailliages* and *sénéchaussées*. It may be observed in passing that there was an extraordinary number of officers of *bailliage* and *sénéchaussée* among those elected, which is perhaps not unconnected with the fact that these areas formed the constituencies. Add to these the various officials of the state services—25—and the total of 278 is reached, that is some 43 per cent of the whole membership.

To describe these men simply as lawyers is to ignore one of the essential features of the *ancien régime*. It would be almost as justifiable as a social analysis which classified the Justices of the Peace in England primarily as lawyers, for as late as the eighteenth century administration and justice were inextricably mixed up in most countries. The great majority of the so-called lawyers were in fact juridico-administrative officers, holding *charges* in municipality or *bailliage* or one of the state services. These were nearly always venal posts, which went therefore to those with a sufficient competence to pay the purchase price, unless they were lucky enough to inherit them from a relation. Thus in 1789 the office of notary would cost as much as 300 or 400,000 *livres* in Paris; in the provinces it might be worth much less.

An office or *charge* was an investment, a status and a job. Those who bought them were not spending their money for nothing; they drew in return a commensurate income from fees. How much work they had to do for it must remain a matter of doubt: the number of officeholders is evidence of the financial needs of the Crown, rather than of the administrative needs of the country. One little *bourg* of 3,000 inhabitants in the seventeenth century rejoiced in a *bailli*, a *prévôt*, a *lieutenant*, a *procureur fiscal*, six notaries, four *sergents*, twelve *procureurs*, and four *greffiers*. Doubtless they also served the surrounding countryside, but it seems a lot. It is difficult not to suspect that, whatever their fees, they were overpaid for their services. They could reply, of course, that having bought their jobs they were entitled to a return on their investment.

The presence of such a large proportion of venal officers in the Constituent Assembly is at first sight difficult to reconcile with the holocaust of their offices effected by the Assembly itself, apparently with little protest. One can understand that they were ready to sacrifice the privileges of the *noblesse* and the clergy, but that an important part of their own income should have gone the same way appears at first sight to indicate a spirit of self-sacrifice and idealism rarely to be predicated of the average political man. We need not, however, in this case hypothesize any superhuman virtue. The venal offices were abolished, it is true, but not without compensation. Admittedly, the compensation was in *assignats:* but no one as yet knew, or dreamed of, the depths to which the *assignat* was to fall. Those who clung to their paper money long enough doubtless lost it all, but it is permissible to suppose that many rapidly reinvested their compensation. It would be interesting to know to what extent the payment for the venal offices was used for the purchase of the nationalized lands of the Church. Certainly the coincidence by which the venal officers, who formed such an important element in the Constituent Assembly, obtained a large supply of free capital, just at the time when an unprecedented opportunity for its investment in land was opened to them, was a very happy one.

It need not be assumed that there were no other motives, of a more disinterested nature, involved in the treatment of the venal offices. But though the demands of a more efficient administration called for their abolition, the venal officers had no occasion to feel that their posts were contrary to social morality. They were all, in a sense, living on the state; but if they looked higher up the social scale they could see plenty who held places and pensions by favour of the Court, without having had to pay for them, or having to do any work in them at all. In their monopoly of the positions combining the maximum of remuneration with the minimum of duties the privileged orders had something more valuable than a mere decorative social superiority and the bourgeois a substantial grievance.

Thiers, who was close to the Revolution and knew many of its participants, held that if the Crown had established some equality in official appointments and given some guarantees, the major source of discontent would have been eliminated. De Tocqueville, a little later, put forward a similar view of the revolution of 1848. "If many of the conservatives," he wrote, "only defended the Ministry with the aim of keeping their salaries and jobs, I must say that many of the opposition only appeared to me to be attacking it in order to get jobs for themselves. The truth, a deplorable truth, is that the taste for official jobs and the desire to live on the taxes is not with us the peculiar malady of a particular party, it is the great and permanent infirmity of the nation itself"—"C'est le mal secret, qui a rongé tous les anciens pouvoirs et qui rongera de même tous les nouveaux."

De Tocqueville, I think, was mistaken only in supposing that this was peculiarly a cause of revolution in France. I suspect that it has a broader application to other revolutions. . . .

. . . One cannot but ask oneself what would have happened to the Revolution in France if in a similar way so many of those who were to be its leaders had in advance been absorbed into the ranks of power and prestige. Whatever else the *tiers état* of 1789 wanted, they certainly wanted *la carrière ouverte aux talents.*

Returning to the analysis of the revolutionary bourgeoisie, it may be said that the Revolution did not end with the Constituent Assembly, and that its subsequent developments brought, in the Convention, another set of men into power. An analysis of the membership of the Convention gives results which naturally vary from those for the Constituent Assembly. The financial, mercantile and manufacturing section is even smaller—83 out of 891, some 9 per cent. Lawyers are present in about the same proportion of one-fourth. Office holders are down from 43 to 25 per cent, though as the venal offices were now a thing of the past, it is unlikely that this figure represents all those who had held such positions under the *ancien régime.* A tiny group of *petits bourgeois* and ordinary soldiers appears, to offset which we have rather more nobles and colonial proprietors. There are more clergy, of course, now that they have no Order of their own. The most notable development is the appearance of a substantial group of what one might call professional men in addition to the lawyers: 32 professors or teachers, some of them also clerics; 58 doctors, surgeons or pharmacists; some lower officers of the army, the navy and merchant marine; a few writers and actors. Altogether this category has risen from about 5 per cent to 17 per cent.

Like the *Constituante,* the Convention is still almost exclusively a bourgeois assembly, and in 1792, as in 1789, bourgeois has to be interpreted in the sense of a class of *fonctionnaires* and professional men. Admittedly, its actions were not the same as those of the *Constituante.* Under pressure from the popular movement in Paris, and amid the storm and stress of counter-revolution and war, policies were accepted by a purged Convention which, as is the way of revolutions, after the purgers had themselves been purged, it was to repudiate. These surface storms of the Revolution are not my subject. When they had died down, and under Napoleon it was possible to make some calculation as to who had emerged in triumph, it could be seen that the smaller fry had mostly continued to inhabit the shallows, while the officials and the professional men of the *ancien régime,* mixed with a fair number of former nobles and a few able men from the ranks, had emerged as the governing class of the new régime.

Once again figures tell the story better than words. Of the members of the Constituent Assembly and the Convention, 111 held high office, and 518 lower offices, under Napoleon, and of these over one-third had held office before 1789. Both Assemblies contained many obscure men who subsequently sank back into the obscurity from which they had emerged. They contained more than a few who, republican by principle, refused to accept the Empire and the share in the fruits of office which they might otherwise have had. There were also the liquidations, the method by which revolutions solve the problem of too many people pursuing too few jobs. But in the end it may have been that a fair proportion of those who had given up their venal offices for compensation at the beginning of the Revolution obtained new ones that were free from the stigma of venality at the end. It may at least be suggested as an hypothesis worthy of investigation that the essence of government in France after the Revolution remained where it had been before, in the great and now renewed bureaucratic *cadres.* With Napoleon returned the *Conseil d'État,* to resume the functions of the councils that had formerly surrounded the throne. Since then, assemblies and Emperors and Kings have come and gone, but the *Conseil d'État* and the *maîtres des requêtes* have remained at the apex of the administrative pyramid and provided the lasting structure of government behind a series of changing régimes.

It may seem that as a result of this interpretation the Revolution is reduced considerably in scope, that everything that survived after 1799 had already been gained by 1791. Essentially this is, I think, true, but how, then, account for eight years of disorder and continuing revolution? One answer that is often given is to attribute it to the struggle against the Counter-revolution. I suspect that this is to give too much weight to a movement that was moribund from birth; but the myth of the Counter-revolution is not my subject here. The war was, I believe, a more important factor, but that also is another subject.

The Revolution began from above, but it was continued by pressure from below. This did not come from the peasantry, who achieved their objective at an early stage and after that ceased to have any active interest in the Revolution beyond safeguarding their gains. But in the towns the poorer population suffered increasingly from inflation and the shortage of supplies, and constituted, therefore, a source of potential unrest which could be exploited by the political factions. If it had been calculated —which of course it was not—for the perpetuation of a revolutionary situation, the system of inflation could not have been better chosen. But when it came to an end the difference between 1799 and 1791 was far less than that between 1791 and 1789.

If I have put forward the view that the interpretation of the Revolution as the substitution of a capitalist bourgeois order for feudalism is a myth, this is not to suggest that the Revolution itself is mythical and that nothing of significance happened in France at this time. The revolutionaries drew a line at the end of the *ancien régime,* subtracted the negative factors from the past, and added up the sum of what was positive, to be carried forward on the next page. A class of officials and professional men moved up from the minor to the major posts in government and dispossessed the minions of an effete Court: this was what the bourgeois revolution meant. The peasants relieved themselves of their seigneurial dues: this was the meaning of the abolition of feudalism. But even taken together these two developments hardly constitute the abolition of one social order and the substitution of another for it, and if the accepted theory is not quite a myth, it seems singularly like one.

Did the Revolution effect no more fundamental change than this? In French economy it might be considered that it held back rather than encouraged changes which were to come much later and are still very incomplete. Politically it replaced the divine right of the King by the divine right of the people. In theory this was to substitute an absolute power for one limited by its nature, and to eliminate the rights of the people as against a government which was henceforth theoretically themselves. The war dictatorship of the Committee of Public Safety, and the Napoleonic Empire, were the historical if not the logical sequel to the assertion of the sovereignty of the people. But this aspect of the Revolution has perhaps been unduly emphasized of late. Sovereignty remained sovereignty, whether exercised in the name of God or the people, even though the Revolution changed both the possessors and the nature of power in the state.

I implied, earlier in this lecture, that the Revolution was not one but many. One of the greatest of its aspects I have so far neglected. Men have ideas, whatever those historians who have tried to decerebrate history may say, and these ideas are not to be treated merely as the expression of material interests. The explanation of the causation of the Revolution simply in terms of the ideas of the eighteenth century has long been discarded from serious history, but this is not to say that the revolutionaries were mere economic animals to be summed up in terms of the stud book and the bank balance, or reduced to a number of holes punched in an index card. The members of the French revolutionary assemblies had been bred on the ideas of the Enlightenment. Reforms such as the abolition of torture in legal proceedings and many other legal changes, or the removal of the disabilities of Protestants and Jews, are not to be explained in terms of material interests. But here again, though the Revolution may have accelerated some of these reforms it perhaps put back others. Here also the historian has to admit not only that these reforms were the children of the ideas of the eighteenth century but that their implementation had already begun before 1789. The reign of Louis XVI was an age of reform, which the Revolution continued. The armies of the Revolution and Napoleon, it has been said, spread the humanitarian ideals of the eighteenth century to the rest of Europe, strange missionaries though they were. There is some truth in this, though if we consider the development of subsequent history we may be tempted to think that the seeds of the Enlightenment, east of the Rhine and south of the Alps and the Pyrenees, fell on very stony ground. The main point I want to make, however, is that whether we analyse the Revolutionary age in terms of social forces or of ideas, it appears more and more clearly as the child of the eighteenth century and only to be understood in terms of the society out of which it emerged. To interpret the Revolution we must look back as well as forward, and forget if possible that 1789 has ever seemed a date from which to begin.

But here I am myself falling into the error of speaking as though there were a single French Revolution, to be summed up in a single formula. This conception, whatever theory it is enshrined in, is the real fallacy behind all the myths of the French Revolution—the idea that there was *a* French Revolution, which you can be for or against. If in some respects the revolutionaries gave expression to the ideas of the Enlightenment, in others they undermined their application; for they stood between the rational and the romantic ages, between the Enlightenment and the religious revival, between a great wave of humanitarian sentiment and the Terror, between the oecumenical ideal and the rise of nationalism, between the idealism of 1789 and the cynicism of the Directory, between the proclamation of universal brotherhood and the wars of Napoleon. They reached the heights of heroism and descended to the depths of civil strife. A whole generation packed with significance for good and evil is summed up in the phrase the French Revolution. We may pick out what we admire or dislike in it and call that the Revolution, but either is a partial verdict. Its significance in the world today is such that we must take all its aspects, for good or for bad, into consideration in our contemporary world-picture. The great school of French historians which has enlarged our knowledge of the Revolutionary age has driven farther away the boundaries at which ultimate disagreement begins; but no single historian, and neither contemporaries nor any succeeding generation, has ever grasped the whole of the Revolutionary age in a single all-embracing view. Every interpretation of the Revolution must in the nature of things be partial, and every partial view is a myth.

PART III: PERSPECTIVES ON THE EIGHTEENTH CENTURY

The French Revolution in the Context of World History

GEORGES LEFEBVRE

Georges Lefebvre (1874–1959), until his death the dean of French revolutionary scholars, first became known with his doctoral dissertation on the peasants in the Department of Nord, which he published in 1924. His international reputation dates from the years after World War II, which saw the appearance of his masterful one-volume synthesis on the French Revolution and on the Napoleonic era. At an age when most men enjoy a well-earned rest, Lefebvre remained an astoundingly productive historian who combined tremendous erudition and thoroughness with breadth of view and of interest.

On the eve of the French Revolution, almost all of Europe was governed by what we now call the *ancien régime*. The prince enjoyed absolute power. The Church looked upon him as God's viceroy and in return he upheld the Church's authority by imposing his religion on his subjects. He had cast aside the concept of natural law, originating with the Stoics and developed during the Middle Ages by theologians like Thomas Aquinas, which assumed a society founded on free contract between governor and governed. Indeed, power had then been conceived only in terms of community welfare and was justified as a guarantee of the inviolable and legitimate rights of the individual.

To achieve absolute power, the prince had undermined seignorial authority and the political authority of the clergy, though allowing them to retain their social preeminence. In becoming subjects, the nobility and the clergy kept their privileges; the king, himself anointed and first gentleman of his realm, did not intend to submerge these orders in the masses. The Old Regime was indeed aristocratic in its structure.

There was a third feature characteristic of France and some other states. In these countries, while the prince had created a territorial and administrative framework, he had not carried this process to its logical conclusion. National unification was therefore incomplete, not only because of the diversity of legal systems, weights and measures, and the customs barriers which

From Georges Lefebvre, "La Révolution française dans l'histoire du monde," *Annales—Economies, Sociétés, Civilisations,* III (1948), 257–266. Reprinted by permission of *Annales*. Translated by the Editor.

impeded the emergence of a national market, but also because the prince had granted or yielded special privileges to provinces and cities. In addition, he granted similar advantages to groupings, usually organized along professional lines, such as the nobility and clergy, so that society was hierarchical and partly "corporative." These estates implied privilege and therefore inequality. Absolutism, relying on "divide and rule," personified inequality . . . and besides, each estate, united by privilege and jealous of its superiority, demanded submission from those lower in the social scale. Nonetheless, the nation, created by submission to a single leader, by ties of material progress, language, and culture, remained divided territorially and socially. Even so, the French were better off than other nations: elsewhere the state, viewed as the personal property of the prince, took no account of national minorities, many of which were scattered among rival or enemy powers.

This regime faced two internal problems that were both political and social. The aristocracy (in other words, the nobility, since the clergy lacked social unity) resented the political impotence to which it had been reduced by the monarch whose power it dreamed of sharing. The nobleman, himself occasionally a victim of despotism, yearned for a freedom consonant with his dignity. This problem was a legacy from the past.

The other problem looked to the future. Ever since the tenth century there had developed a new class based on commerce, industry, finance, on personal rather than on landed property. This new bourgeois class had emerged from the Third Estate in a society in which land, as sole instrument of production, had entitled its owner to seignorial authority over those who farmed for a living. The king had drawn on these bourgeois both for money and officials, and they came to enjoy not only wealth but education and culture as well. Since the Renaissance, moreover, the new rationalism, exemplified by recent empirical science, provided an intellectual orientation consonant with bourgeois interests. Capitalism, which in its beginning phase had enjoyed mercantilistic state patronage, spread beyond the bounds of commerce to industry. The introduction of machinery opened such unlimited horizons for the bourgeoisie that the profits enticed even aristocrats to join in the exploitation of the world.

The bourgeoisie sought to obtain some share of power and therefore was willing to ally itself with the aristocracy against the king, yet bourgeoisie and aristocracy also were in opposition to each other. For centuries the middle class had striven for nobility; though this objective had not been altogether abandoned, the aristocracy was becoming more exclusive at the very time that the middle class, greatly increased in numbers, could no longer hope for mass ennoblement. The bourgeois, therefore, went beyond the nobles' demand for power and freedom to claim the end of all privileges as well as equality before the law.

At the end of the eighteenth century, because of the unequal pace of economic development, these problems appeared in a different guise in the various parts of Europe. Central and eastern Europe, which had long been backward by west European standards, did not partake in the new maritime trade routes and the exploitation of the New World which the great discoveries of the fifteenth and sixteenth centuries had opened up. The gap between East and West thus tended to widen. In this eastern and central European area newly-formed large states had adopted mercantilist policies and relied on the bourgeoisie for economic development and political organization. These states practiced what has been called "enlightened despotism." The mercantile middle class was, however, small in numbers, and the Enlightenment had more substantial influence on government officials, professors and writers. The prince also confronted a threatening aristocracy. In Poland this nobility had seized power, while in Sweden only the *coup d'état* of Gustavus III had prevented a similar eventuality. In Hungary and Belgium the aristocracy had fought Joseph II to a standstill. In Prussia and Russia the monarchy had compromised, the aristocracy trading obedience and submission to the ruler for a free hand in dealing with their peasants whose serfdom, as one moved east, approached slavery.

In the countries of the south, particularly in the Iberian peninsula, the Counter Reformation had impeded free intellectual development. While Italy had been bypassed by the great overseas discoveries, Spain, in any case poorly endowed by nature, had been ruined by war. The nobility was somnolent, while the bourgeoisie grew only slowly. The peasant, as in France, did enjoy royal protection.

The maritime nations, Holland, England and a newcomer, the United States, offered a striking contrast to these land-based states. All of the former were Protestant. Holland and England had been the greatest beneficiaries of the rise of the European economy since the sixteenth century. In Holland the bourgeoisie was in control of the republic despite the nobility's support of the monarchist ambitions of the House of Orange. Since in this struggle neither constitutionalism nor liberty was at stake, it may be argued that a compromise between these three forces had either been reached already or was at least within sight.

While Holland had long been regarded as enjoying the greatest degree of freedom, the fame of the English and American revolutions, Britain's power and brilliant intellectual contribution made the Anglo-Saxon countries favorite antitheses to the absolutist regimes.

In England an aristocracy that enjoyed few privileges and no exemption from taxes differed markedly from its counterpart on the continent. Above all, only the lords formed a distinct legal estate, yet even their prerogatives were passed on to their eldest sons only. The younger children were commoners on a level with the gentry and squires who were represented in the House of Commons. The lords themselves could scarcely trace their genealogy beyond the Tudor era, since the nobility had been decimated by the massacres of the Wars of the Roses; hence they were not far removed from their middle class origins. Above all, however, since England was an island, the military character of the nobility had become attenuated or had disappeared altogether, to the point where military service was merely a matter of personal inclination. Consequently nothing stood in the way of the nobleman, even of the peer, going into business, and the distinction between the upper middle class and nobility was only a matter of ancestry and the kind of prestigious distinctions which were even within reach of the bourgeoisie. Nowhere else was there such social mobility: money alone defined class lines. The maritime and colonial expansion had consolidated a community of interest between the aristocracy and the capitalist middle classes. The Reformation, by sanctifying the struggle for naval and world supremacy waged against Spain and France, had heightened this solidarity. After the Catholic and Francophile Stuarts had, in the course of the seventeenth century, succeeded in rousing the whole nation against themselves, two revolutions had insured the final defeat of royal despotism. Yet neither the aristocracy nor the upper middle classes had directed their alliance against the monarchy as such. The Revolution of 1688 was a compromise establishing constitutional government which balanced king, lords, and a combination of gentry and middle class in the House of Commons. The latter was elected by a limited franchise which by its very lack of system insured the absolute control of the wealthy.

History was a source of precedents to be used against royal despotism. More than once the aristocracy had succeeded in extracting concessions from a monarchy that had appeared all-powerful since the Norman conquest, the most famous of these concessions being Magna Carta. English liberties were founded on such precedents and customs, in short, on tradition rather than on philosophical speculation. Even so, natural law had not been forgotten. It inspired Locke's justification of the Revolution of 1688. The importance of his works, which served as bible of all the continental *philosophes* of the eighteenth century, can hardly be exaggerated. However, once the Whig oligarchy had gained power, it gradually abandoned Locke as its intellectual mentor, since the contract theory, the recourse to natural right, could also justify democratic movements which loomed on the horizon threatening its power. On the eve of the French Revolution, Burke agreed with George III in considering the British constitution to be the most perfect imaginable. For Burke the constitution recognized not the rights of man but the rights of Englishmen: only the English had been able to conquer these liberties and they alone had clear title to them.

Not only did English liberty make no claim to universality, but the English state itself did not grant complete freedom of thought. Even though, like Holland, England enjoyed broader toleration than Catholic countries, the state religion was maintained. More important, equality before the law had never become a fighting issue. Because the aristocracy was allied with wealth, the upper middle class had never had to appeal to this equality. Political freedom had never undermined a determination to maintain the existing social hierarchy.

Anglo-Saxon America did not have to become quite so empirically minded. Natural right remained a vital force in these Puritan communities that had left Europe to escape, not only religious intolerance, but the weight of despotism and of aristocratic society. In breaking with the home country, the colonists appealed to natural right to justify their secession, while their declarations proclaimed the rights of man, not merely the rights of Americans. Their public law reflected this universality of natural law. At the same time the Protestant sects sought to safeguard their independence by insisting on religious liberty. There were, however, notable limitations: no one claimed any rights for colored men, and slaves remained slaves. Freedom of thought was not the rule and even though state and church were separated, it was taken for granted that religious liberty was confined to Christians. As in England, there was no insistence on equality. As the United States had never had peers or privileged persons the issue of privilege had never divided gentlemen and rich bourgeoisie. There were gentlemen descended from the British gentry who, living as noblemen on their plantations in Virginia and other Southern colonies, ruled over their enslaved blacks. Among these were the men who, like Washington, led the War of Independence and governed the republic during the first decades of its existence. However, men of a very different social background, such as Jefferson, had also become planters. Nothing prevented a Benjamin Franklin, printer turned merchant and journalist, from taking his place on the outer fringe of the ruling elite. Equality before the law for all whites, irrelevant as an issue in the struggle against Great Britain, had thus never been raised, nor was it ever considered a challenge to a social hierarchy based on wealth. Actually this equality before the law did not extend to politics, since the state constitutions restricted the franchise. What was called "democracy" in France during the first months of the Revolution was a government belonging not to the ruler or the aristocracy but to the nation. The actual procedures allowed, however, for the dominance of the moneyed class.

The English and American examples exercised a profound influence as the birthplaces of freedom. America, moreover, had stressed the universal validity of natural right. In practice this equality of rights, however admitted in principle, was not wholly applied, and in any case was not the basis for these revolutions. It is understandable that the example of these countries should have swayed not only the middle classes but also the continental aristocracy opposing royal power. For both, liberty seemed the pertinent catchword. Since equality had not been one of the consequences of these revolutions, it did not occur to the continental aristocracy that liberty might endanger its social predominance.

The Anglo-Saxon revolutions had been directed against absolutism in behalf of a bourgeois-aristocratic alliance. The French Revolution was to be a very different affair.

From the socioeconomic as well as the geographical point of view our country occupied an intermediate position in Europe. Just as in other continental states, intermittent warfare had helped the nobility to preserve its military character. The very fact that this nobility faced impoverishment only increased its exclusiveness and its tendency to become a closed caste. Yet as a maritime nation France had also participated in European colonial expansion: its commerce was second only to that of Great Britain, while its industrial capitalism, though backward in comparison to the latter, nonetheless enjoyed the most advanced development on the continent. The French bourgeoisie, though closer to the land than the English middle class, was infinitely larger and more influential than that of any other continental monarchy. Perhaps most peculiar to French society was the important role played by saleable offices. The king had tapped middle class wealth by putting many official positions on the auction block. In order to increase their saleability or to gain the support of the officeholders, the king had endowed some of these positions not only with corporate privileges but even with personal or hereditary nobility. Just as in England, the infiltration of bourgeois families meant a renewal of the aristocracy. By the eighteenth century few nobles could produce a genealogy going back to the Crusades. This new nobility of the robe was establishing an increasingly intimate relationship to the military nobility. Nonetheless the nobility of the robe was not only businesslike in the management of its own affairs, but also kept up contact with other officeholders who had not graduated to the nobility. It also maintained ties with a socially less prestigious group, namely the lawyers. An intermediate class had thus developed which included these nobles at the top with officeholders in the middle, and commoners at the bottom. As a result of common professional outlook it shared the concept of law, of a legal order, of a monarchy whose prerogatives were limited by the sovereign courts' privilege of registration and remonstrance. Within this class a quite Cartesian rationalism and a tradition of the monarchy governing in cooperation with the wellborn and the well-to-do found special favor. Locke's ideas of natural right had fallen on fertile ground. In this respect, too, France occupied an intermediate position. While the absolute monarchy did cooperate with the Church in thought control, in contrast to Spain, Italy and Belgium, the Counter Reformation had not succeeded in stifling the development of philosophy and scientific inquiry. Finally, the French king had not had to yield power to the nobles; unlike England where a dominant aristocracy had uprooted the peasantry by enforcing enclosure, the majority of France's peasants were for all practical purposes free landowners.

Down to the time of the Fronde, the French nobility had often countered royal power with armed resistance. Even at that time the judicial officeholders had shown that they too could resist the monarch's authority. This reappeared once the hiatus imposed by Louis XIV was over, although its nature had altered as society had evolved. By the eighteenth century, armed outbreaks had become obsolete: the sovereign courts relied instead on a bourgeois appeal to public opinion, to constitutional tradition, to natural right. At the same time the aristocratically-dominated provincial estates played an increasingly important administrative role, particularly in

Languedoc and Brittany. The office of *intendant* was preempted by nobles, as were the bishoprics. Commoners, already excluded from the sovereign courts, in 1781 were barred from becoming professional officers, though they could still be promoted from the ranks. Aristocratic theorists, among whom Boulainvilliers and Montesquieu stood out, justified seignorial power by claiming that the aristocracy was descended from the Germanic conquerors of Gaul. Peasants complained over what historians have called the "feudal reaction," namely the increasingly exacting collection of manorial dues. It is clear, in any case, that some great landed proprietors benefited from royal ordinances permitting them to enclose land and to divide the commons. It is customary to concentrate on the eighteenth century growth of the bourgeoisie and the rise of the Enlightenment which reflected its aspirations. This period, however, was equally notable for the growing influence of the aristocracy, who attacked royal authority and successfully resisted all reform attempts that would have undermined their privileges, particularly exemption from taxation.

The French Revolution, in its first phase a revolution of the nobles, represented the climax of this rebirth of aristocratic opposition. By September 1788 when Louis XVI had been forced to call the Estates General, an aristocratic triumph seemed in sight. If, as anticipated, the Estates were to meet in three separate orders with the clergy dominated by the aristocratic episcopate, the nobility would be in control. This nobility was willing to help the king bring order out of financial chaos, but only at the price of certain concessions.

What were these concessions? The aristocrats demanded what they called liberty, that is, a constitutional government relying on regular meetings of an Estates General dominated by the nobility. In the provinces they would displace the *intendant*.

The nobility had no inkling that it was undermining the bulwark of its own privileges by weakening royal power. The nobility did not foresee that once the Estates had been called, the bourgeoisie would find its voice. Much as in England, the price of their cooperation was likely to be equality of rights. When this price was demanded the French nobility refused to make this concession. As a result the Estates General, intended as a battering ram against royal authority, saw the nobility thrown back on the defensive. A second phase of the Revolution had begun—the bourgeois revolution.

When Louis XVI accepted both freedom and constitutional government on June 23, 1789, some of the national objectives seemed to have been met. When, however, he threw his support to the nobility and clergy, this was tantamount to rejecting equality which henceforth became the crux of the struggle.

Actually the king, by means of his army, seemed capable of ending the conflict on his own terms. The artisans and peasants, however, whose own interest was unmistakable, supported the bourgeoisie. The popular and peasant revolutions, culminating in the night of August 4, broke the power both of the monarchy and the nobility. Unlike the bourgeoisie which had not aimed for the ruin of the aristocracy, the popular revolution wiped the slate clean and soon completed the social revolution by nationalizing church property.

In practice the consequences of this social revolution were not carried to their logical conclusion in 1789. A part of the manorial dues had to be redeemed; the Catholic clergy retained its monopoly of public religious services, its state financial support, its control of marriage, education and welfare work. When the aristocracy and the monarchy looked abroad for support, civil war broke out. This civil war persuaded some of the middle classes to throw in their lot with the lower classes to complete the destruction of the aristocracy by confiscating the *émigrés'* property and by seeking to crush the clergy's influence. In these circumstances the revolution turned democratic: it adopted manhood suffrage, proclaimed a republic, freed the slaves, separated State from Church, and secularized education, welfare and personal status.

This is the way in which the French Revolution gained its distinctive place in the history of the world. Although the revolution appealed to natural law (as the American Revolution had also done), its achievements left a universal imprint quite alien to British liberty. Its sheer momentum, moreover, was much greater. Not only did the revolution establish a republic but it insisted on manhood suffrage. Freedom for whites was not enough: the slaves were freed. Not content with toleration, the revolution admitted Protestants and Jews to full citizenship and, by secularizing personal status, recognized the individual's right not to belong to any religion.

All this, however, was secondary to the real mission of the revolution which was to be the revolution of equality. While in England and America the alliance of aristocracy and upper middle class had precluded a stress on civil equality, in France the bourgeoisie had been forced to emphasize it by the unbending attitude of the nobility. Indeed, by abolishing manorial rights, the peasants initiated equality with a vengeance. Since by revolutionary definition liberty was tantamount to obedience to lawful authority alone, liberty and equality were complementary in that liberty by itself would lead to privilege for the few.

In gaining freedom and equality, the French had become the Nation One and Indivisible. This new interpretation of national sovereignty is a third outstanding characteristic of the revolution from which grew France's claim that nations, like individuals, should be liberated. Thus France claimed Alsace, Avignon and Corsica by appealing to free consent rather than to conventional treaties between rulers. International law was being revolutionized just as internal civil law had been. In this early phase the revolution looked forward to peace and cooperation among free nations united by the ideal of a society of nations, even of a universal Republic.

These characteristics explain the French Revolution's impact on the world and its long-range significance. At the same time, although these principles have since registered gains, it would be a mistake to attribute their dissemination solely to the revolution. The example of England and the United States had certainly not been forgotten. It would be equally false—and this is a widespread idea—to credit this ideological expansion solely to the magnetism of ideas: in areas adjoining France, the *ancien régime* fell victim mainly to the revolutionary armies led by Napoleon. Since that time capitalism has become the chief vehicle by which these new principles have conquered the world. These principles, as historians have sought to show during the last several decades, reflected the interests of the middle class who championed them. In granting economic freedom, abolishing serfdom, freeing the land from the burden of tithe and manorial dues, bringing church property back into the dynamic channels of the economy, the bourgeoisie was paving the way for capitalism. Wherever capitalism has penetrated—and thanks to its inner dynamic it has become ubiquitous—the same kinds of transformations have occurred. By strengthening or creating a middle class, capitalism has helped the triumph of liberty and civil equality as well as the development of nationalism, in our own day even among colonial peoples once dominated by the white man.

Nonetheless the French Revolution has retained an emotional drawing power unrelated to any selfish interest. It is associated with popular insurrection symbolized by the storming of the Bastille and the wars of liberation which the *Marseillaise* commemorates. This is the work of those who died for the revolution. To ignore the influence of class interests and economics on a movement of ideas would be a mutilated history. To forget that the bourgeoisie was convinced that its rise was identified with justice and the welfare of all mankind would be no less of a distortion. The fighters of July 14 and August 10, the soldiers of Valmy, Jemmapes and Fleurus risked their lives not from self-interest but because they enthusiastically embraced a universal cause.

Nonetheless this equality of rights, this essential principle of the French Revolution by which the bourgeoisie of 1789 rationalized the abolition of aristocratic privilege based on birth, had some unexpected consequences. The middle class, confident in its ability, power and prospect, had ignored the ill-tempered warnings of its opponents in this respect.

For this middle class, as for the Anglo-Saxons, equality meant equality of opportunity. Although everyone was free to take advantage of these opportunities, obviously not everyone had the requisite ability. What significance could freedom of the press or free access to public office have for someone who was illiterate? Yet public instruction was contingent upon being well-off if not actually wealthy. The bourgeoisie of 1789 interpreted the right to vote and to be elected in a similar spirit. This right, like others, required certain prerequisites, in this case the payment of a given amount of taxes as evidence of a certain standard of economic independence. Thus the rights of man and of the citizen, formulated by the bourgeoisie, were to remain largely academic and theoretical. There was little doubt, and none after Thermidor, that in the eyes of the middle class only property owners were entitled to actual, as against theoretical, power. Property being hereditary meant that privilege due to birth had not, as counterrevolutionaries observed, been eliminated after all. Democrats were soon to point out that private ownership of the means of production led to the subjection of the wage earners. Private property in workshops, the sole source of employment, made illusory the rights of the propertyless.

The lower classes, aware of these implications, had always opposed economic freedom which led to capitalism and the triumph of big business. Their ideal was a nation of peasant proprietors and independent artisans. In any case they sought state protection for the wage earner from the omnipotence of the rich. In order to gain power and organize the defense of the revolution after August 10, 1792, the republican bourgeoisie had accepted universal suffrage and continued its alliance with the so-called "sans-culottes." This alliance resulted in a compromise between the middle class aspirations of 1789 and the masses who called for government intervention to secure a more widespread distribution of property, public education for all, economic controls to keep prices and wages in balance, and a minimum social security system. This policy of "social democracy," initiated by the Mountain during the Year II, horrified and frightened the bourgeoisie and seemed to be banished forever after 9 Thermidor. When, however, republicanism reappeared after 1830, some of its followers took up Montagnard principles. With the re-establishment of universal suffrage in 1848, the application of these principles became one of the facts of political life.

Even during the revolutionary period, however, some groups had gone even farther by calling for the abolition of the private ownership of the means of production and the creation of a communist democracy intended to fulfill the promise of equality. This same intention has, in the final analysis, also made socialist theoreticians, particularly in France, present their systems as the completion of the French revolutionary achievements left unfinished by the middle classes. This is not to claim that the tradition of the French Revolution is the sole element in this development. Religious and humanitarian feelings have also been instrumental in aiding social progress. Above all, the transformation of the economy has had a powerful influence on the broad extension of equality of rights. The victories of capitalism led to trade union and political organization of the proletariat made possible by the concentration of business and labor, which defined and accelerated the class struggle. These organized elements could not be ignored. At the same time, the phenomenal productive growth engendered by capitalism, by increasing the resources available to human society, has brought a variety of welfare services, such as education and social security, within the realm of feasibility, whereas during and long after the revolution the cost of such services relegated them to Utopia.

Leaving aside differing approaches to history, the fundamental problem of our contemporary world appears to be the problem of equality within each nation and equality among nations. It is not the historian's job to prophesy how mankind will resolve such a problem; yet the historian can attest that the French Revolution not only raised this issue but also indicated various directions in which a solution might be sought. One may conclude, therefore, that, admired or loathed, the name of the French Revolution will long remain on men's lips.

The Advent of the French Revolution in Retrospect

MARTIN GÖHRING

Martin Göhring, a professor at the Institute for European History, University of Mainz, is the foremost contemporary German interpreter of the French Revolution. His massive *History of the Great Revolution* has been hailed as a substantial new synthesis based on an acquaintance with the archival sources. Professor Göhring's approach, which tends to view the revolution from the vantage point of the Old Regime rather than that of the post-revolutionary era, may reflect the historian's earlier studies in the institutional history of seventeenth- and eighteenth-century Europe.

An old world had collapsed, marking the end of an epoch in the midst of the most violent upheavals which were also the birth pangs of a new era. Without this stormy prelude the Great Revolution would have been inconceivable; yet what made it possible, what had caused the disintegration of the Old Regime? However often these questions have been posed, they have received a variety of answers—answers that have frequently been no more than simple-minded formulas. Yet such world-shaking events do not have simple antecedents that can be neatly and clearly illustrated. The historian Mathiez explained the overall pattern of the revolution in terms of an antithesis between everyday reality and legal fiction, institutions and *mores,* the letter and the spirit. It took at least a century for these contradictions to come to a head, requiring the interaction of all kinds of circumstances, the intervention of a variety of intellectual, material, universal, as well as purely human, forces. . . . Great political achievements are not gained by a fluke but must be won. One need only examine English history to note the endless succession of struggles which accompanied its growing freedoms.

. . . The last of the French kings laid claim to far greater power than any other ruler in Europe, while being less capable than any monarch of translating this claim into workaday reality. Such was the malformation of the ancient monarchy which had achieved its existing structure by an evolution characterized by repeated ebb and flow. Kings and ministers again and again sought prestige until they overextended their power and were succeeded by paralysis and exhaustion, permitting the restoration of opposing forces. The weight of French absolutism rested far more on personality than on institutions, so that the state was only intermittently imbued with absolutist doctrines. When in the final phase these doctrines had altogether ceased to be fruitful, the eve of the Revolution saw the utter confusion of popular sovereignty, royal absolutism, feudal power, corporate privilege, customary and Roman law, Estate-administered and centralized provinces.

From Martin Göhring, *Geschichte der Grossen Revolution* (Tübingen, 1950), I, pp. 380–403. Reprinted by permission of J. C. B. Mohr Verlag. Translated by Dr. Melvin Cherno and the Editor.

In the last analysis the absolute monarchy was toppled by forces with which it had been contending since the Middle Ages, because at the height of its power the monarchy had neglected to uproot these potential opponents. It is indeed remarkable that the state should have been undermined by those who in the nature of things should have been its most distinguished champions, yet it has never been sufficiently stressed that the revolt of the privileged orders was the basic precondition for the Revolution itself. In overthrowing absolutism, they gave the middle classes an object lesson in sedition and made insurrection respectable. Absolutism was forced to bow, not to a liberal spirit, but to conservatism or even reaction. This is a fundamental postulate from which everything else must be derived.

From a long-range historical perspective, the revolution of the privileged which began with the Assembly of Notables in 1787 was the culmination of an aristocratic reaction rooted in the opposition movement in the latter part of Louis XIV's reign, which prevailed throughout the eighteenth century. . . . From the time that the judges of the high courts . . . had justified their opposition to governmental edicts as a right that was "a characteristic feature of the constitution," political activity had become polarized. The unity of the spiritual and political world, so essential to absolutism, was irretrievably lost when the king was no longer the embodiment of the whole nation. There was a parting of the ways between state and nation, as the latter became a distinct concept and gained self-awareness. Ever since the bankruptcy of Louis XIV's system, the claim "l'Etat c'est moi" had become a fiction.

The elite of the sovereign courts, entrenched in an almost unassailable position against royal claims to power, were not only able to curb effectively the legislative authority of the crown, but were also paramount in furthering the nation's self-awareness. They claimed a mandate founded on the deliberately misleading analogy of parliament and the Estates General to back up a position which only such parallels could justify. The sovereign judges and their publicists revived the sixteenth-century dogma of popular sovereignty based on a monarchy limited by Estates which was henceforth never again forgotten by the French people: France became politically conscious in the process. The sovereign courts and their prerogatives were also chiefly responsible for perpetuating in the name of freedom the bizarre and checkered administrative chaos that kept France weak by blocking administrative unity. As bulwarks against the extension of the crown's power, they enjoyed popularity. Their stubbornness may further be credited as leading to the point where every serious attempt at reform on the part of the government was viewed either as unconstitutional or as despotic violence, until the prevailing form of government itself was viewed as despotic. And finally, under the continuous barrage of criticism unleashed by the courts, the regime lost all semblance of justification. . . .

The courts' usurpations could only be countered by extraordinary means—by rescinding the offices or arresting the office-holders; in the name of personal freedom and the sanctity of private property the judges declaimed endlessly against despotism. In this way these slogans were gradually adopted by the people. The courts' long-winded remonstrances, padded with discussions of political theory, nonetheless enriched speculation about politics, fiscal policy and administration. By constantly referring to national aims and rights, they awakened the nation's desire to participate in politics. Their ideological influence was heightened rather than undermined by the qualities for which the *philosophes* reproached them: their intolerance, bigotry, ignorance, their blind attachment to the past, their exclusive response to self-interest and prejudice. . . .

. . . One may say, however, that the process of disintegration set in when Louis

XIV, sidetracking the unique opportunity for governmental reform provided by Colbert, overreached himself in senseless violation of his subjects and all sound principles of government. By carrying out his system *ad absurdum,* he thus provoked criticism. The continued decline provided a moral justification for the opposition which was reinforced not only by its own traditions but by the example of England. One of the roots of the Great Revolution which should not be overlooked is the widespread Anglomania which created real political ferment.

Fundamentally Frenchmen were very conservative, in the eighteenth century as well as today. While no one wanted what we would call a revolution, everyone sought change, some general stabilization which would be particularly welcome to the holders of government bonds. This is quite natural in a state constantly on the verge of bankruptcy. A state which time and time again had reneged upon its obligations . . . could hardly expect great loyalty from subjects facing a continual threat of bankruptcy. This question came to the fore particularly during the last decade of the Old Regime. Anxiety over property values, always a potent stimulus to mass action, mobilized those Frenchmen who were creditors of the state. When state finance and private wealth are so closely connected, the creditor will demand some guarantee of the security of his capital from the debtor. The citizen's vital interest in the state thus originated in an essentially practical endeavor. The continued preoccupation with questions of governmental reform was to lead to a more generalized discussion of the constitution.

The government itself contributed to this trend by seeking time and time again to cast off the restrictions which bound it and to secure by means of reform a greater leeway for action. The government justified this attitude in extensive introductions to its edicts that appealed to broad principles; it hired publicists and writers to attack both abuses and the opposition [to reform]. In this way some of the basic questions of political life were opened to discussion, shaping the development of a public opinion. That public opinion became a real power may be attributed chiefly to government policy, as can be seen in Turgot's attempt to enlist the nation against the government's opponents. For Necker public opinion was a god to be worshipped on bended knees, as evinced by the calculations which entered his *Justification* and the impact which that document made. What a catastrophe, nevertheless, were this power of public opinion to turn against the regime!

The Enlightenment broadened and completed this process. By stressing [that the decadence of the government preceded the Enlightenment] we deny the claim that the political theorists of the eighteenth century—particularly its outstanding spokesmen Montesquieu, Voltaire and Rousseau—consciously prepared the Revolution. . . . They were fundamentally different in their outlook on life, their mental equipment and their orientation. From the political point of view . . . they embodied three distinct worlds agreeing only in the common rejection of the *status quo*. Insofar as all three were critics, they were bearers of the Enlightenment; yet at least as far as Montesquieu and Voltaire are concerned, this did not make them revolutionaries. As to Rousseau, for twenty-five years the *Social Contract* which earned him his revolutionary reputation was looked upon as a Utopian fragment. Other political writers, like the Abbé Mably, who during their lifetime enjoyed a greater reputation than Rousseau, were more radical and inflammatory. None of them, however, had created the climate of opinion of the eighteenth century; they had embodied, or at most explicitly spelled out, prevailing currents of opinion. The *philosophes* merely expressed what men thought; if some among them gained fame, this was because they were better and more persuasive writers than others. . . .

Ideas have power. A decadent government confronted by a youthful, dynamic ideology faces a difficult position unless the established power neutralizes threatening ideas by adapting them to its own use. Yet how did French absolutism react? Alternately the regime embraced or rejected the new spirit; alternately writers were granted pensions or imprisoned; alternately unauthorized publications were winked at or suppressed by arresting some poor bookseller on whom fell the full severity of the law. . . .

There loomed an unbridgeable chasm between the spirit of the regime and that of the age. What could be more degrading and hateful for men who have reached full maturity to face restrictions on their freedom and development! What could be more unbearable for the man of letters than to know that his intellectual attitude might bring down upon him a warrant of arrest, a *lettre de cachet*. At the same time, what could be more burdensome for a regime than to claim control over the private life of the individual, who needs autonomy if he is to develop a true morality and reach genuine fulfillment? Only immature peoples would subject themselves to such infringement. What the seventeenth century man had accepted as a customary burden roused the man of the Enlightenment to indignation.

Yet Frenchmen were . . . conservative even while they shared the outlook of the Enlightenment. Neither their elevated style of life nor their fine manners predestined them to be revolutionaries. Their political aim was merely a government capable of realizing the new ideals by reconciling the needs of the state with the demands of society, in harmony with the spirit of the times. Such a government would have respected certain basic rights of the individual and granted freedom of self-expression. There were such governments, which presented a great contrast to French absolutism and as such constituted the most genuine threat of the Enlightenment. While France wasted its strength in fruitless attempts to achieve reform, outside of France the new intellectual outlook prevailed and became politically potent. We need merely consider little Prussia with its efficient, centralized system of government, its sober and thrifty administration, its sound finances, its rising standards of living, its progressive policies in the realms of agriculture, welfare and religious toleration, its large-scale planning, its judicial safeguards, etc. Here was a state to serve as model of culture and legality for its age. Its monarch, himself considered a leading intellectual, showed consummate skill in reconciling the identity of king and state by applying the principle that the monarch be the first servant of the state.

One might also turn to Austria which, thanks to the reforms of Empress Maria Theresa, was assuming a modern guise. Its ruler lived up to the basic dictum of the Prussian king, though she started from a different intellectual premise. One might pay special attention to the thoroughly enlightened Joseph II, who began the transformation of his state in harmony with the spirit of his age, deliberately imitating the King of Prussia. Starting in 1780 Joseph undertook a revolution from above by centralizing and bureaucratizing his administration and struggling against corporate authorities, privileges and immunities. With firm hand, he nationalized the most powerful of the corporate bodies, the church, by dissolving its ties to Rome and integrating it as a subordinate department of the state. He had smashed the power of the church by secularizing its extensive properties and dissolving hundreds of monasteries. The training of the clergy was supervised and spelled out. In an attack on superstition processions and religious festivals were abolished. He proclaimed freedom of conscience, securing it by an edict of toleration. In all areas he encouraged enterprise: by rescinding monopoly rights; by granting the right to enter any trade or profession, as well as by recognizing the claims of free labor. He undertook a generous land reform by abolishing serfdom, granting land to the peasants and giving them legal protection from their landlords who were deprived of their seignorial monopolies. Forced labor was reduced, dues in kind regulated. On state-owned lands deliveries in kind and forced labor were transmuted into cash payments, while the breakup of great estates and the secularization of church property was meant to encourage the formation of a peasant middle class. At the same time Joseph II pursued a new tax policy founded on the principle that everyone was to shoulder his share of the public burden according to wealth and income, regardless of social status. What encroachments and transformations in the realm of public affairs!

Joseph accomplished his gigantic task without consideration of protest and opposition, with a contempt for prejudices and customs surpassing that of Frederick the Great. A thoroughgoing physiocrat strongly influenced by Turgot's theories, Joseph carried through in Austria what Turgot and his collaborators had labored in vain to accomplish in France. Beyond Austria proper, this enlightened reform of the state extended to the Austrian possessions in Italy, namely Lombardy and Tuscany. In Piedmont-Sardinia, in the meantime, the liquidation of the feudal system, initiated by Charles-Emmanuel III in 1771, was being completed under Victor Amadeus in 1778. Even the autocratic Tsarina Catherine II paid homage to the Enlightenment by corresponding with the great minds of the time. An open admirer of Montesquieu, she invited Diderot to her court and basked in the praises of the *philosophes*.

Thus the world of the European states altered and became more modern, confirming Voltaire's epigram: "Peoples are what their rulers and ministers make of them." Where was France in this competitive race among governments? This nation of twenty-five million people, this fertile land with its varied resources which had once ruled Europe, had become almost a second-rate power as the result of its political stagnation and enervation. As minor powers of yesterday ignored France in dealing with major European questions, embittered Frenchmen pointed to their government, their king, their court as the guilty parties. As one contemporary put it, to trace the decline of France to political insignificance is to write the history of the Revolution—a judgment which contains a good deal of truth. The judgment of the historian Sagnac is thus corroborated: the Revolution became necessary because the government was incapable of undertaking the reforms carried out in other states. . . . It became the task of the sovereign nation, by a precipitous and convulsive effort, to catch up with and overtake the development reached by other states, yet basically the program involved was derived from enlightened absolutism. Much of this program, constitutional aspects excepted, was already contained in "Josephism" which was nearly identical with physiocracy. One may thus conclude that the Revolution had been consummated in men's minds before it became a political reality.

The significance of this process of transformation was underlined by an event which took place outside of Europe, exerting a strong influence on intellectual developments: the uprising of the American colonies against their mother country, England, and their union in an independent state. Among the educated this realization of their professed ideals evoked a powerful response when they contemplated the organization of a society founded on such eternal principles as natural right and the basic rights of men. This was the spirit in which the Americans wrote their constitutions and created their governments.

The events in America assumed a unique significance for France. The French monarchy, based on absolutism and divine right, had espoused the alien cause of the rebellious colonies by intervening and decisively contributing to their victory. France sent soldiers, received American envoys who were feted and venerated as heroes of the history of mankind. This did not prevent the French "freedom fighters" from returning as the heralds of the new ideals, irreconcilably opposed to the political conditions of their homeland. Thus motivated by its enmity toward England, by the urge to humiliate this rival, France committed what amounted to political suicide. . . .

The germ of the revolutionary contagion would have proved harmless for France had the French contribution simply drained off excess resources, since a reasonably healthy state would not have been endangered. The political system faced its greatest threat when, as direct result of the American war, the financial situation took a catastrophic turn. Indirectly and directly the war required the outlay of hundreds of millions, covered by bond issues which during the war years amounted to 900 million and 300–400 million in subsequent years. These loans compromised the financial situation irretrievably, since the deficit increased enormously and the state debt rose to such an extent that more than half of all receipts had to be allotted to interest charges: 250–280 million out of 475 million. If another seventy million is subtracted for the admitted expenses of the court, there would have been little left for any other administrative need. Considering the financial and credit conditions of the times, only basic reforms could prevent catastrophe.

Can one say that the American war caused the Revolution? To answer in an unqualified positive would be to confuse cause and effect. The same could be said of the Assembly of Notables which was called only to avoid conflict with the sovereign courts. This was, moreover, the motive which had led Necker to rely on a policy of borrowing money in order to carry out the interventionist policy in America, a policy which strained the financial resources of the state though it would have been within the means of the people. The crux of the matter was that national wealth could only be tapped inadequately because the system of taxation was defective. It was defective because the practices and principles of taxation reflected the inorganic and ailing structure of the state itself. This itself was the effect of objectionable principles, prejudices and shortsighted fiscal practices, culminating in the nonsense by which the rich used their wealth to escape taxation, while the burden borne by the poor varied inversely with their poverty. These guidelines of internal policy had prevailed throughout centuries, thus reflecting the basic features of the general policy. In this whole chain not one link could be attributed to chance. . . .

All this indicates how difficult it was to reform the state, since such reforms would have required interference in depth, immense exertion and creativity. How often in the course of two hundred years did France possess a government capable of such efforts? The best that could be expected ever since the second half of Louis XIV's reign was an above-average minister now and then, who would be stymied by administrative inertia, by jealous colleagues and a corrupt environment. Under Louis XIV the unity of the government was at least maintained and the absolutist system kept its doctrine intact. But thereafter unity disappeared: secretaries of state assumed regal authority within their departments without the slightest regard for their colleagues' policy. Ministerial authority prevailed as long as it enjoyed the favor of the king's mistress and of the court, unless the minister were ousted by the intrigues of the corporate bodies or by some other plot. . . . This was particularly true of the most important ministry, the Comptroller Generalship, which was the hub of internal policy. What a waste of experts this practice entailed; it was understandable that finance ministers of stature had the shortest term of office. By forcefully pushing the reform measures which the ever-recurring emergencies demanded, they made themselves the target for the opposition. The determined opposition of the court alone was enough to topple a minister. . . . If leadership were to come from the crown it would have required a monarch of the ability of Henry IV to recognize the problems of the age and capture the loyalty of the nation. The prevailing contempt for the person of the king resulted from the fateful failure of the last three Louis. In certain circles it henceforth became almost a disgrace to admit serving king or state. One well-known contemporary characterized this growing lack of respect, which reflected the change in people's attitude: under Louis XIV no one dared to speak; under Louis XV they whispered; under Louis XVI they spoke up without restraint. . . .

Then as now, judgments are a matter of comparison. What contrast between the last two French kings and the Prussian king, or even the rulers of Austria! The dissipated, immoral and irresponsible Louis XV divided his life between his mistresses, hunting and merry-making; Louis XVI, though sober and virtuous, was also the worst conceivable representative of a regime symbolized by the person of the king. Lacking any political sense, intellectually as well as physically nearsighted and clumsy, Louis XVI feared responsibility yet proved incapable of subordinating himself to anyone eager to shoulder this burden. The greatest portion of his time was spent in hunting—between 1775 and 1789 about 1560 days—unless he was busy moving his household or following his unkingly hobbies; the least of his time was devoted to public business. Both French kings began their day at ten or eleven o'clock, since the ceremonial of getting up and breakfasting required hours. The rulers of Prussia and Austria, on the other hand, buried themselves in their work and their concern with the welfare of the state and of their subjects. Even the aging Frederick the Great's workday never began later than five o'clock.

The kings of one country subjected themselves to duty; those of the other relied on their divine right. Yet how could divine right remain a vital idea when it was embodied in such rulers? . . . Even the church challenged divine right. The Throne derives power from its alliance with the Altar only so long as the church dominates or at least directs intellectual movements. When, as was the case in France, the Altar renounces and betrays its mission and the cassock is used to exploit the idea of the divine, the alliance becomes a curse. The spirit of the age would never have become so powerful had the church enjoyed inner vitality and remained the true guardian of the faith. The opposition which it evoked would never have grown so strong if the church had not sunk to the level of an institution solely concerned with its corporate demands and special interests, to the detriment of the public weal. . . .

What was true of the church as one of three Estates of the realm was no less true of a nobility that had become an obstacle and opponent instead of fulfilling its normal role of supporting and serving [the state]. How can one ultimately account for this? The responsibility rests with the monarchy which over a long period degraded the concepts which alone make a viable corporate society possible. . . . The monarchy had denied the claims stemming from personal achievement and proclaimed instead the prerogatives of birth and money, the supremacy of privilege in every form.

One may wonder how it was possible for a regime to vegetate so long in the absence of substantial support. Tocqueville's explanation may be considered: the monarchy's organization offered the means to crush any individual opposition, while the opposition of the whole nation could normally be ruled out, since the kings had gained their power by playing class against class. . . . To overthrow absolutism took but one moment of unity; divide and conquer had thus been the ruling practice of French absolutism. . . . The prevailing class conflict, which stemmed from the nefarious system of privilege, was the . . . fatal flaw of the French nation: the lack of any sense of loyalty to the state, the predominance of selfish interests. No state can last if its achievements fail to awaken and continually renew its subjects' loyalty. . . .

The class consciousness of the bourgeoisie, reflected in its need for self-assertion, sharpened the opposition. In the realms of culture and economics, the eighteenth century had a markedly bourgeois character. Only in the political sphere was the bourgeoisie impotent, particularly in France. Yet until the opening of the eighteenth century the middle class had been a source of great strength to the monarchy. From its ranks new men were drawn into the ruling elite, which thus invigorated it. With the help of the middle class . . . the monarchy had achieved power. Under Louis XIV the bonds had loosened; after him this tradition of cooperation disappeared as the state became feudalized. The ruling class became exclusive, demanding proof of established nobility as a prerequisite for army and administrative posts. Thereafter the purchase of a noble title could only serve as a token of distinction or as a means of obtaining privileges. Social as well as political conditions thus shaped the demands for liberty and equality: freedom of the individual, of speech, of economic enterprise; equality before the law, of rights and duties in public life, of access to all offices—hence an end to all discriminatory practices and privileges.

To transform a decadent system and to infuse new life into a corrupt ruling class has always been among the more difficult political problems. . . . This is where French absolutism failed; with it foundered the monarchy's historic mission of building organically a unified national state with a single law code and equal rights. . . .

The last, decisive thrust of [French] absolutism came too late and was launched from an unfavorable position with inadequate troops. An absolutism which commanded neither confidence nor faith lacked all means to cast off the bonds which shackled its power, bonds that had been forged by its own irresponsibility, short-sightedness and intellectual decadence. . . .

We have outlined the complex of causes of the Great Revolution and indicated the interaction of the causal factors. It has been shown that the basic causes were rooted in the political and social conditions of the *ancien régime,* from which the intellectual movements also sprouted. . . . In this last rearing-up of the feudal world, the gates of the new epoch were thrown open. This reaction was not a purely French movement: it was seething in Austria where the conservative classes in Hungary and in the Netherlands were soon to rise against the reforms of Joseph II. It would have gone against the whole trend of historical development if absolutism had been overthrown only to be replaced by reactionary forces. . . . Yet the struggle was essential if the new world, whose embryo was the man of the Enlightenment, was to be born. This was the stake of the struggle over the Estates. Everything hinged on the make-up of the Estates General, on whether the deputies of the Third Estate were to equal those of the nobility and clergy and whether they were to meet and vote as one body. A positive decision would have insured the triumph of the national forces, while a negative would possibly have given the privileged orders an all-encompassing vote for all time—alternatives which explain the bitterness of the conflict.

Without compulsion individuals and whole corporate bodies do not surrender long-held privileges or give up claims to power that appear on the verge of realization. Such self-abnegation is even less likely in behalf of a class over whom leadership and tutelage is claimed. Yet it is also natural that classes that have reached maturity and self-awareness should not continue to accept humiliation and discrimination once the force of circumstances relents. The moment for a social transformation had arrived. Beginning with the debate on the organization of the Estates General and the applicability of medieval precedents, men turned to discuss the constitution, the nature of authority in the abstract, of the existing authorities, and indeed the nature of society itself. The dynamic of politics, growing out of the interplay of opposing interests, led men to turn to the present. Reason, rather than historical precedent and tradition . . . became the court of last appeal. From the re-evaluation emerged new concepts of the state, society and nation. . . .

French, Western, or Atlantic Revolution?

R. R. PALMER

Together with Godechot I share the view that the revolutionary period has been studied too exclusively within a national framework. A broader perspective does entail certain dangers. Obviously the French Revolution was in a real sense unique, a point which I shall discuss later. While it is true that each nation does have its peculiar identity, to overvalue this identity, to attach a special importance to this impenetrable *Eigentümlichkeit,* is symptomatic of a philosophy of German origin which the Germans themselves are trying to discard. It is true that each country has its distinctive ethos and way of life, an idea which is particularly attractive to the English who don't like being put on the same plane with other people.

In order to undertake comparative studies, a greater unity is needed in which the parts are related to each other in terms of their similarity, difference or interaction. We find such a unity in the concept of an occidental civilization—or, particularly for the eighteenth century, a European civilization, provided America be included. As for myself, I attach little importance to the adjective "Atlantic" even though it points to two facts which I deem of capital importance: that access to the ocean had accelerated the development of western Europe by bringing into existence a variety of classes, including a new and more enterprising bourgeoisie of a type scarcely known in eastern Europe; and, secondly, that the colonial world of the Americas, including the United States at the time of their independence, enjoyed fairly intimate and significant relations with Europe. I do not insist on the word "Atlantic" since I have no intention of ignoring eastern Europe merely because it is cut off from the sea. In fact, like the Polish historian Lesnodorski, I even perceive similarities between the Virginia planters and the Polish nobles with their serfs, their lands, their literary traditions of an agrarian republic, and their revulsion against taxes, cities and a central government.

In order to write the history of a whole zone of civilization, common features, problems and tendencies must be isolated, even though in different places social conflicts may have varying outcomes. The common trait of the eighteenth century was the aristocratic character of government and society. This aristocratic orientation is most clearly perceived in the institutional history of what I call the "constituted bodies" of the eighteenth century: the parliaments of Great Britain and Ireland, as well as those of the provincial estates in France; the diets, state councils and assemblies that could be found all over Europe west of Russia; the governors' councils in the Anglo-American colonies. The economic basis for a majority within these bodies was landed property, even for the greater part of the members of the House of Commons in England. The mainstay of the Estates of the United Provinces, the governing council of Geneva or a minority within the

From R. R. Palmer, "Révolution française, occidentale ou Atlantique?" *Bulletin de la Société d'histoire moderne,* série 12, vol. 59, Bulletin spécial (1960), pp. 2–7. Reprinted by permission of the Comité de la Société d'histoire moderne. Translated by the Editor.

House of Commons was revenue from banking and commerce. All, moreover, drew substantial income from their political positions. It may also be said that, regardless of the source of their wealth, these élites were more and more recruited by birth, by family and by hereditary succession. They were thus in the process of becoming increasingly oligarchic and exclusive.

The phenomenon of an aristocratic resurgence or of the pressures from a hereditary upper class became evident in many countries in the eighteenth century. To cite but a few bits of evidence, it is certain that the British parliament and the Prussian bureaucracy were more aristocratic at the end than at the beginning of the century, that the revolts of the Belgian Estates and the Hungarian Diet against Joseph II raised the question of domination by privilege, and that the same problem came to the fore in France when the Estates General gathered in May 1789. Similar indications may be found among the churches. Quite recently one of my students, Mr. Norman Ravitch, undertook a statistical analysis of the social origin of bishops in France and England. He found that in France the proportion of bishops whose nobility could be traced back two hundred years or more rose from fifty-three per cent for the reign of Louis XIV to eighty per cent for the years preceding 1790. In the Anglican Church, an establishment naturally quite different from the Catholic Church in France, the proportion of bishops born to the peerage or the gentry rose from thirty-six per cent during the reign of Charles II to sixty-three per cent during the last thirty years of George III's reign.

Our common master, the late Georges Lefebvre in his essay, "The French Revolution in World History," viewed the French Revolution as the revolution of equality. This same concept may be extended to the movements in other countries during this same period. Almost everywhere demands were being made in behalf of equality of rights in the face of privilege.

At this point a few words about the American Revolution are called for, since the latter has been subject to some misapprehension in France. Lefebvre himself contrasted the French Revolution with what he called the "Anglo-Saxon" revolutions, a term by which he lumped the American Revolution with the English revolutions of the seventeenth century. I would like to point out that the term "Anglo-Saxon," though still common in France, has been little used in America for the last thirty years. It is true that the forms of American and British government have a common origin, but this origin goes back further than the eighteenth century. The American Revolution did not conform to the English norm; while the latter had been a revolution by parliament against the king, the American Revolution was directed against parliament, with King George III playing a basically minor role. In the English revolution the landed classes had come to power, while the Americans shook off the domination of this English landed class which had acted through parliament and the colonial governors. The American Revolution resembled the French more than is generally believed in being a revolution of equality. Obviously this is a generalization which has its exceptions and limitations. The colonial aristocracy of Virginia and other states remained fairly strong. Since slavery, which weighed more heavily than the serfdom of eastern Europe, was maintained, equality only went into effect within certain limits. Even so, and while confessing that American historians are themselves in disagreement over this point, it seems obvious to me that the principle of equality was furthered by the American Revolution. At the start equality meant no more than legal equality between America and England, or between the colonial assemblies and Parliament. It soon became necessary to go beyond this. While the pre-revolutionary aristocracy was largely silenced or expelled, in the new state governments the governor and his council were made into elective offices. The Massachusetts constitution of 1780 [for example] provided that the governor, senate and house of representatives be elected for one year only by popular and direct franchise, a franchise in which the great majority of adult males participated. This was no English eighteenth century idea; the underlying concepts, the national character, was undergoing a transformation. Admiration for a hierarchical society, so widespread among all English classes during this period, became something exceptional in the United States. There is no getting around the fact that Americans set up liberty as their ideal, symbolized by the law which required that the word be inscribed on every American coin. Yet our liberty could include equality, particularly equality of opportunity, as may be seen today in the context of the question of Negro-White race relations. Alexis de Tocqueville was right in claiming equality rather than liberty as the dominant principle of the United States. I invite my French colleagues to re-read Tocqueville and to study the American Revolution.

In any case this revolution had an immediate impact on Europe. I have tried to describe it in my book and in a chapter of the new *Propyläen-Weltgeschichte* which has just appeared in Germany and whose editor views the influence of the American Revolution as ushering in the modern period. It is true that this influence was felt because of conditions prevailing in Europe and above all in France. One may even say that France created this influence by glorifying the American Revolution. There has sometimes been talk of an "American mission" by which America supposedly assumed the task of leading the world toward democracy and peaceful progress. Don't blame this solely on Americans! A German scholar, Otto Vossler, maintained thirty years ago that the French taught Americans to see themselves in this universal light as liberators of humanity. The French, he asserts, invented the American mission, handing it over to Americans just as a hundred years later they built the Statue of Liberty and donated it to be erected at the entrance to the port of New York.

The American Revolution had three kinds of consequences. It intensified the sense of a new era which became manifest during the century of the Enlightenment. It heightened the desire for equality (or the resentment against inequality), especially on the part of the middle class with regard to the aristocracy. There is ample evidence to this effect. I merely cite a curious poem, *Voyage in America,* written in 1786 by L. G. Bourdon, secretary-interpreter at the Ministry of Foreign Affairs. He dreamed of America as though it were the promised land.

Where greatness does belong to him,
Not by the accident of birth, nor whim
Of rank, but by a virtuous and decent mien:
In usefulness alone is greatness seen.[1]

Thirdly, the debate over America, particularly in France before 1789, popularized constituent assemblies, written constitutions and declarations of rights, examples first furnished by America which were soon to find a more spectacular realization in France.

It is well known that unrest, if not revolutions, had occurred in a number of other countries before the French Revolution. I believe that here too the principles of equal rights and of secularization played a central part. Everywhere there were protests against the powers held by narrow, oligarchic or hereditary groups. England and Ireland in the years from 1780 to 1785 witnessed the climax of the movement for "parliamentary reform." One should not be misled by the word "reform" which reflects the habits of moderation in English politics. More was at stake than "reform" in the usual sense of the word, though admittedly until the Irish uprising of 1798 the amount of violence would not have justified the use of the term "revolution." However, the "reformers" were, as had been the case

[1] Où sans distinction de naissance et de rang,
L'homme le plus honnête et le plus respectable,
Le plus utile enfin, soit toujours le plus grand.

of the American revolutionaries, generally very hostile toward parliament. They had more in mind than an extension of the franchise, since the modern concept of suffrage, not to speak of its extension, was yet to be created in England. The dispute ranged over the whole theory and nature of representation and political authority. Presbyterians and Catholics made up the opposition in Ireland while in England the Dissenters played a prominent role among the reformers, recalling the privileged position enjoyed by the Anglican Church. In Holland and Geneva a middle class excluded from public life fought a governing bourgeoisie. In the Austrian Netherlands, at first the Estates opposed the Emperor in an aristocratic reaction; later a democratic group, labelled *Vonckist* by its enemies, struggled against the privileged estates. In this instance the old line bourgeois of the guilds and the few privileged cities, together with the nobility, clergy and peasantry formed a sort of conservative party. In contrast, the new middle class—bankers, wholesale merchants, lawyers somewhat removed from landed and governmental power—became the leaders of a democratic opposition. In Sweden similar divisions existed, but here the king upheld the middle class against the nobility in 1789, only to be assassinated by a few noblemen three years later. In Germany, to be brief, politics was still a branch of journalism, while in Italy the new forces were alive but did not act until the arrival of the French in 1796. In Poland and Hungary, in the absence of an indigenous middle class and a free peasantry, politics was confined to noble landowners and a small number of intellectuals and was further complicated by nationality problems. In these countries the lower nobility entered into a struggle against an aristocracy of magnates. The Polish revolution and the constitution of 1791 did make a few concessions to the middle classes with respect to equality of rights which, though trifling by western standards, might have made a revolutionary impact east of the Elbe.

It should be underlined, however, that all these movements failed outside of America and even there the revolution, in my opinion, would not have succeeded without French intervention. The French Revolution and these agitations and abortive revolutions shared common aspirations to equality and secularism. While such similarities have some significance there is nonetheless a great difference between an idea and its realization. In the British Isles the parliamentary classes sidetracked reform. In Holland the Orangists suppressed the Patriots, thanks to British and Prussian intervention. In Belgium the Estates crushed the democrats before being themselves crushed by an Austrian restoration. The Polish revolution was smothered by Prussia and Russia in alliance with a few Polish magnates. All these events marked the victory of the old order over the new forces, to the accompaniment of much conservative theorizing. The main ideas of Edmund Burke had already found expression by 1784, not as a reaction against the French Revolution but against the modernization of the British parliament. The counterrevolution preceded the French Revolution. The principle of anti-revolutionary intervention made famous by Metternich a generation later was already in operation at Geneva in 1782, in Holland in 1787, and in Poland—as in France—in 1792. The same language was being used: "The cause of all legitimate governments," it was said, was threatened "by the atrocious and unprovoked horrors of sedition." This was the way in which a Genevan patrician complained about the turmoil in his native city in 1782 when he appealed for international intervention against the burghers of Geneva.

Before turning to the French Revolution, I would like to consider some comments by Jacques Godechot and others, who find that my ideas, too narrowly anchored to politics, neglect the economic and social structure. They claim further that I have ignored the population crisis and that, while furnishing a fairly clear description of the aristocracies, my picture of the democrats is hazy. I am grateful to these careful readers and admit some validity in these strictures. Allow me a few words in response.

The eighteenth century aristocracy was something that was already in existence while the opposing movement, democratic insofar as it clamored for equality, was in the process of being born. Since the aristocracy was already embodied in an institutional structure, it may be described in concrete terms. The "democracy," if I may be permitted to use the expression, was in the process of assuming form. It was an *anti*-movement, a mixture of discontents. One must avoid false precision in treating a thing so imprecise in itself, and I therefore hesitate to link it too closely to one or several classes defined in economic terms. As to the demographic crisis, the effects of a rapid population growth will vary according to circumstances, technological levels, means of production, boom or depression in employment, not to speak of political and psychological factors. Population increased very rapidly throughout Europe and even Asia during the eighteenth century. Population pressure on the land existed just as much in the Kingdom of Naples as in France, yet it was in France that a peasant revolution took place. There was a horrible *Jacquerie* in Hungary in 1790 but it did not result in a revolution. Probably the population crisis had a less ambiguous impact on the upper classes in France and elsewhere. It would seem that positions in governments, armies and churches increase less rapidly than does population. An accelerated population growth produces a high proportion of young people seeking careers. The competition of aristocratic and bourgeois families for the available desirable jobs might intensify the aristocratic resurgence as well as middle class demands for equal access to office.

Social and economic structures cannot be clearly separated from politics. If the means of production and the forms of income influence governments, the possession of political authority, military power, office and jurisdiction may also determine social classes and economic institutions. The problems of public life may be viewed from a religious perspective in the sixteenth century, from an economic viewpoint in the twentieth, and from a political vantage in the eighteenth centuries. It seems to me that, on the whole, politics carried the day during the eighteenth century.

In any case, social structures are not entirely missing from my book. I have brought out, for example, that the English landed aristocracy shared common interests with the middle class in terms of its capitalistic ideas of production and sale and that parliamentary reform failed because the new industrialists did not yet lend it their support; that the Dutch Patriots were weakened by lack of popular mass support; that in eastern Europe, serfdom, the lack of cities, of a middle class and of national homogeneity left few resources at the disposal of the revolutionary leadership.

What should one say, finally, about the French Revolution? M. Marcel Reinhard worries that the specific characteristics of the French Revolution may be lost or diluted in a vague "Occidental Revolution." He discovers an inclination to minimize the importance of the French Revolution, or to reduce it to a "minor episode" within the framework of a general history. This has certainly not been my intention.

On the contrary, it seems to me that when the French Revolution is viewed in conjunction with a contemporary world movement its unique characteristics stand out more clearly than ever. The aristocratic resurgence, which prevailed almost everywhere, produced a revolution in France because of the power of the opposing social forces, namely the French peasantry and middle class. I continue to follow Lefebvre who contended that the characteristic feature of the French Revolution was the concurrence of four revolutions: a revolution by the aristocracy, by the middle class, by the peasants, and by the urban masses. Revolution means conflict and in France all of the social forces were more dynamic and powerful than anywhere else, hence the inevitability and tremendous scope of the conflict. The French state was the most populous in Europe and was second in wealth only to England. The aristocracy, one might say, was more aristocratic than elsewhere, the Church more closely tied to the upper classes, the middle class more numerous, wealthy and alert. Sharply differentiated in their living standards French peasants were readier to free themselves from the seignorial regime, while the masses in a city like Paris were more responsive to action at the moment of crisis. In short, the alliance of peasants and bourgeoisie, however transient, made the Revolution of 1789 possible, just as the alliance between the revolutionary middle class [Montagnard], the lower classes and the *sans-culottes* preserved and furthered the revolution a few years later. Such alliances would have been inconceivable anywhere else.

Despite my awareness of the ubiquity of revolutionary agitation, I agree with M. Reinhard in believing that during the eighteenth century France alone underwent a revolution in the fullest and most profound sense of the word. Only France carried out a revolution solely by its own means and under its own power. I would not even make an exception of the American Revolution which required French assistance. As for the Batavian, Helvetian and Italian revolutions which took place in the last years of the century, described by Godechot in his *La Grande Nation,* the success of the native revolutionaries in these countries was made possible by France. Where French aid failed, as was the case in Poland in 1794 or Ireland in 1798, attempts at revolution failed. Only in France did the aristocracy meet with successful resistance before 1792. France became the leader of an international coalition of revolutionaries with sympathizers throughout Europe and America in a vast movement against the international aristocracies which had gained the support of Throne and Altar. It should be evident therefore why I believe that this viewpoint in no way minimizes the importance of the French Revolution.

French Revolution or Western Revolution? The Second Phase: 1789–1815

JACQUES GODECHOT

Jacques Godechot, professor of history at the University of Toulouse, has been one of the most eminent French scholars in the field of French revolutionary history. Even though he has also written on such topics as a history of the Atlantic and of Malta, he is best known for his institutional survey of France during the revolutionary and Napoleonic eras and for his brilliant *La Grande Nation,* which treats the expansive aspects of the French Revolution. More recently he has published a history of the counterrevolution viewed as an international movement.

Robert Palmer has shown in what light the revolutionary movement of the years 1770 to 1789 should be viewed. For the period following, I would like to deal with the problem which Robert Palmer and I have already broached in a paper read in 1955 before the International Congress of the Historical Sciences in Rome and which I have also explored in my book *La Grande Nation,* as well as in my *Counterrevolution.* Was the revolutionary movement in Europe and America between 1789 and 1815 a direct outgrowth of the French Revolution, or were the revolutions in France and elsewhere parts of an even vaster revolutionary movement which I propose to label "Western" or "Atlantic"? . . . The former interpretation represents the classic, the traditional view, espoused by historians such as Von Sybel and Albert Sorel. The latter point of view is less novel than is commonly believed, since it was implicit even in the title of Camille Desmoulins' famous newspaper, *Revolutions of France and Brabant.* Barnave expounded a similar interpretation in his *Introduction to the French Revolution,* which has recently been re-issued. He wrote: "It would be impossible to evaluate the great revolution which has just shaken France as an isolated phenomenon. The history of adjoining states and the whole evolution of the last few centuries must be taken into account." Barnave showed that the socioeconomic evolution of all the countries of western Europe was pointing toward revolution. . . . Jaurès, in his *Socialist History,* noted in connection with Barnave's *Introduction* that, "One cannot really speak of a French Revolution but only of European revolution which reaches its climax in France." Numerous statesmen of the revolutionary period, both French and foreign, shared this opinion. . . .

I have no intention of restating in this paper what I have tried to show in several books. I will confine myself, first of all, to a summary of the facts supporting the

From Jacques Godechot, "Révolution française ou révolution occidentale? La deuxième phase: 1789–1815," *Bulletin de la Société d'histoire moderne,* série 12, vol. 59, Bulletin spécial (1960), pp. 7–10. Reprinted by permission of the Comité de la Société d'histoire moderne. Translated by the Editor.

broader interpretation of what we shall call Western revolution. In the second part of this paper, I shall deal with the arguments which have been advanced against this point of view and seek to refute them.

I. THE FACTS

No one denies that revolutionary movements also occurred outside of France between 1789 and 1815. These movements have been explained as the results of planned or unplanned French revolutionary propaganda; others maintain that there was no connection, or that the French Revolution exerted but a slight and remote influence.

For the sake of clarity, the following distinctions should be drawn: on one hand, there were outbreaks which preceded any French military occupation. In these instances it may be relatively easy to distinguish the role played by propaganda from that of local circumstances. We shall also, on the other hand, deal with revolutions which followed upon the arrival of French troops. While in such cases the impact of French propaganda is undeniable, it remains to be seen to what extent such propaganda merely served as a catalyst activating a pre-existing movement.

1. The following revolutionary developments may be included under the first of the above classifications: the creation of political clubs and societies in England from 1789 to 1794, followed by the mutiny of the Channel and North Sea fleets in 1797; the Irish outbreaks culminating in the violent insurrection of 1798; the Genevan revolution which began with the vote for the new constitution of 1791. The climax was reached in Geneva in 1794 with the creation of a revolutionary government complete with revolutionary committee, whose tribunal condemned eleven nobles to death. Undeniably, these events were revolutionary in nature, paralleling the French Revolution and no doubt influenced by it. It is equally certain, however, that these outbreaks were linked to earlier revolutionary attempts, in the case of England and Ireland to the great movements of 1781–1783, in that of Geneva to the revolutions of 1768 and 1782. These earlier movements were in turn connected with the growth of the Enlightenment and the struggles between aristocratic corporate bodies and democrats which took place in much of Europe and North America between 1770 and 1789, and which R. Palmer has so brilliantly analyzed.

The various incidents, the clubs and plots which have been noted for Germany, Hungary, Austria and Italy for the years 1790 to 1796, also fall into this first category. While in these cases the French Revolution also played its role of example, stimulant and catalyst, yet the policies of the enlightened despots and the resistance to them on the part of aristocratic bodies also were at the root of the trouble. Elsewhere the struggle was carried on by a substantial segment of the middle class, and in some areas (Styria, Piedmont) even of the peasantry, against an aristocratic reaction. Even though all these outbreaks had met with violent, and usually bloody, governmental repression, a seed had been planted which would germinate upon the arrival of French troops. Nonetheless, the chances of success of these various movements were more or less minimal because of a social structure differing greatly from that of western Europe. In Hungary, for example, where a small nobility lorded it over a mass of serfs in the absence of any substantial bourgeoisie, the revolutionary movement, confined to the nobility, . . . did not stand a real chance.

The Hungarian conspiracies bear comparison with the revolution in Poland, since the two countries had comparable social structures. The fact that there was revolution rather than conspiracy in Poland may be explained by its political traditions. Even so, this revolution bore only a slight resemblance to what took place in the West. Although the 1790 revolution succeeded in strengthening royal power and granting a few concessions to the middle class, serfdom was left untouched. The movement of 1794 was chiefly a national uprising against the three powers that had invaded Poland. While there was talk of peasant emancipation, the revolt was crushed before any democratic measure had in fact been passed. New ideas had indeed been voiced and a tradition created; yet despite these national peculiarities, the Polish revolution is part of the great revolutionary movement.

The same may be said of the revolutions directed by the Spanish colonies of Central and South America against the mother country between 1810 and 1814. While it must be granted that the question of Indian and Negro emancipation was never raised, the Spanish-American insurgents nonetheless acclaimed the same ideas that had triumphed in the United States in 1783 and in France in 1789. We are thus dealing here with a whole series of revolutions in which French influence is remote and indirect.

2. The opposite is true of the revolutions which followed the arrival of the French armies. Such is the case of Belgium and the Rhineland in 1792 and 1794, of Holland in 1795, of Italy . . . between 1796 and 1799, of Switzerland, Malta and Egypt in 1798. The French role differed from country to country. Wherever there had been previous outbreaks as was the case in Holland, Belgium, Romagna, Naples and some of the Swiss cantons, the French did little more than give assistance to local "patriots." Elsewhere—and Egypt furnishes the most notorious example—they imported a complete, prefabricated revolution. In the long run, the impact of these various revolutions varied proportionately with the degree of local participation: Belgium, Holland, Switzerland and Italy are specific cases. There was, it should be noted, no mechanical connection between French invasion and revolutionary upheaval. The occupation of the northern provinces of Spain in 1795, for example, did not bring revolution in its wake, since local resistance forbade any such move. In 1807 it was also true that the counter-revolution and its directing organ, the Cortes of Cadiz, were more directly responsible for the changes in Spain than was the government of Joseph Bonaparte.

This, then, is the impressive mass of facts indicating that in much of Europe and America the field was clear for the organization of a new regime based on liberty, greater equality, and a refurbished social structure.

II. WHAT ARGUMENTS HAVE BEEN ADVANCED AGAINST THESE FACTS?

* * *

1. First of all, the authenticity of these movements has been questioned. But for the French Revolution no outbreaks would have occurred, so the argument runs. This line is difficult to sustain with regard to the revolutionary movements in Great Britain, Ireland, Geneva and Poland, all of which were clearly linked to events prior to and independent of the revolution in France.

A revolutionary movement is the product of gradual, subterranean economic changes as well as of powerful ideological forces. Indeed, how is it possible to believe that such a movement should respect the arbitrary and superficial lines which we call frontiers? The economic changes of the late eighteenth century were western, not national, as were even the periodic economic depressions, to judge from the limited information available to us. Furthermore, population growth did not halt at the borders, while even censorship could not materially hamper the flow of ideas. The fact is that the revolutionaries were committed to a concept of universal revolution, which, though not universally put into practice, affected all areas where there were substantial revolutionary nuclei.

2. Some who admit that such revolutionary nuclei did exist have nonetheless argued that, except in France, such groups constituted no more than an infinitesimal minority. The revolution was therefore, they submit, essentially French despite its universal trends.

I would answer by asking whether even in France the revolutionaries constituted a majority. The distinctive feature of the revolution in France, accounting as it does for its great initial successes, is the alliance of a powerful bourgeoisie with a numerous peasantry against the privileged in order to smash the feudal system. While no doubt these same conditions did not prevail everywhere, the circumstances in the Rhineland, Belgium, some of the Swiss cantons, and Romagna were very similar. In all areas where the ground had been prepared, the revolution did take root.

3. The institutions which were developed in these countries, it has been asserted, were no more than carbon copies of French institutions and lacked any element of originality. As I have demonstrated in *La Grande Nation,* local revolutionaries frequently did alter these French models to suit their own unique circumstances and needs. This certainly applies to the constitutions, and my own conclusions have been corroborated by Carlo Ghisalberti's notable recent study of the Jacobin constitution [in Italy].

4. It has also been brought out that the position of the Catholic Church in southern Europe, being much stronger than in France, would have prevented any revolution. This is valid for Spain, where, despite the French invasion, revolution not only failed to take place, but where it was the Church itself which organized the resistance movement in 1807. In certain regions of Italy, however, the Church was as much weakened and divided by "Jansenism" as in France.

5. This leads me to an important problem, namely, the geographic and chronological limits of the revolution. As to the latter, to date the beginning around 1770 is unlikely to start a debate. While no doubt the English revolutions of the seventeenth century exerted considerable influence on the revolution of the late eighteenth century, they were, nonetheless, separated by a peaceful interval of eighty years. The terminal date may be more controversial. 1815? Yet the revolution continued in Latin America, while in 1830 the revolutionary embers flared up again. Even 1848 may be looked upon as a continuation of 1789. By contrast, the generalized reaction of 1849 marked a real change. The great popular movements which sought liberty and equality were succeeded by national movements, which, though still drawing upon the revolutionary heritage, were led by monarchs. The outbreak of new popular movements in Russia in 1905 and, on a larger scale, in 1917, looked primarily to the east. The chronological limits also help to define the geographical limits. From 1770 to 1849 immense areas remained unaffected: Russia and European Turkey, almost all of Asia and Africa. While Poland and the Balkans, which were touched by the revolution, may not quite belong to the "Western World," they did nonetheless respond to western stimuli. During the period from 1770 to 1849, the United States, England and France served as models both for revolutions and for institutions. This is why I deem the two adjectives "Western" or "Atlantic" as the most appropriate descriptions of this movement, even though I am aware of their limitations.

6. Why not label this revolution "bourgeois" or "capitalist," as has been suggested? It seems to me that these two descriptions are not fully adequate. Can the Polish revolution of 1790 really be called "bourgeois"? On the other hand, the Meiji restoration did promote the capitalistic development of Japan after 1863. Moreover, the western revolution began, not with a bourgeois or capitalist phase, but with the offensive of the privileged orders against the reforms sponsored by the sovereigns. Under these circumstances a geographic label appears more to the point.

CONCLUSION

I thus suggest that the great movement which overthrew the social, economic and political order of most of Europe and America between 1770 and 1849 should be described as "Western" or "Atlantic." While France and the United States played a preponderant role in this upheaval, its scope was broader. Indeed, this is corroborated by an examination of the counterrevolution, whose greatest spokesmen were not French but included . . . an Englishman, Burke; a Swiss, Mallet du Pan; and a Piedmontese, Joseph de Maistre. The counterrevolution, like the revolution itself, was also [international and] western.

SUGGESTIONS FOR ADDITIONAL READING

Compared to other significant problems of historical interpretation, relatively little has been written that bears directly upon the problem of the Western Revolution of the eighteenth century. There are at least two major reasons for this dearth. The emphasis on the international character of the eighteenth-century upheaval, while a commonplace during the seventeen-nineties, has only been revived quite recently and did not receive an elaborate, full-dress presentation until major works by J. Godechot and R. R. Palmer appeared in the nineteen-fifties. Secondly, opponents of the Western interpretation have stressed national peculiarities over international common denominators. Not unnaturally, they have concentrated on revolutionary histories and monographs written within a national framework rather than book-length rebuttals of the Palmer thesis. By the very nature of their case, therefore, historians stressing the national characteristics of revolution may appear parochial compared to the grandiose generalizers. To avoid onesidedness broad generalizations should be substantiated by national or even local studies of revolution against which overall syntheses should be tested.

The proponents of the international interpretation of eighteenth-century revolutions stress their debt to the analysts who lived through the events. A number of such contemporary accounts are worth reading or dipping into if only to recapture the original flavor of the argument. Among counterrevolutionaries who viewed the revolutions as a world movement, two accounts stand out. J. Mallet du Pan's *Considerations on the Nature of the French Revolution* (London, 1793) is a brilliant analysis by a Genevan ex-liberal turned counterrevolutionary propagandist. Unlike Mallet du Pan, the Abbé A. de Barruel represents uncompromising reaction, not only against revolution, but against the whole Enlightenment. His *Memoirs, Illustrating the History of Jacobinism,* 4 vols. (London, 1797-1799) develop at tedious, yet fascinating, length the thesis of a worldwide conspiracy by *Illuminati* and Free Masons who are behind all political unrest. On the revolutionary side, J. de Barnave's *Introduction à la Révolution française* (latest edition, Paris, 1960) is almost unique for its time (though it was not published until the middle of the nineteenth century) in presenting a materialist interpretation of history. Barnave attributed the revolutions to the material and social development of society, a development which had progressed further in France than in other western countries, accounting for the greater intensity of the French Revolution. The Marquis de Condorcet, on the other hand, in his *Outline of an Historical View of the Progress of the Human Mind* (London, 1795), written while in hiding during the Terror, rested his case on the intellectual progress of the western world, which had reached its highest point in France. Two interesting dissenting opinions from this "Western" approach are found in President John Q. Adams' *Discourses on Davila,* written in the seventeen-nineties, but not published (and then anonymously) until 1805, and F. Gentz's *The French and American Revolutions Compared* * (Gateway, 1959). Both writers made a sharp distinction between the American Revolution, which was legitimate because it took tradition and experience into account, and the French Revolution, which was unjustifiable because of its essentially anti-traditional Utopian aims.

The only comprehensive interpretation of the eighteenth century which has incorporated the western interpretation of revolution without making this the central

* Obtainable in paperback edition.

issue is R. Mousnier and E. Labrousse, *Le XVIIIe Siècle: Révolution intellectuelle, technique et politique* (Paris, 1953) in the "Histoire générale des civilisations" series, a brilliant account which has unfortunately not been translated. By far the fullest statement of the thesis of the Western revolution is R. R. Palmer's persuasive *The Age of the Democratic Revolution,* vol. I (Princeton, 1959), which surveys not only most of the major revolutionary disturbances between 1760 and 1791, but also deals with aristocratic reaction and the enlightened absolutism which paralleled the revolutionary movement. J. Godechot's *La Grande Nation: L'expansion révolutionnaire de la France dans le monde de 1789 à 1799,* 2 vols. (Paris, 1956), shares Palmer's viewpoint, but concentrates on French military and ideological expansion in the borderland during the French revolutionary decade. The same author's more recent *La contre-révolution, 1789–1804* seeks to describe the opposition to the French Revolution in terms of an international movement. Both authors have also collaborated on a paper read before the Tenth International Congress of Historical Sciences in Rome entitled "Le problème de l'Atlantique du XVIIIe au XXe Siècle" (*Relazioni del X Congresso Internazionale de Scienze Storiche, V,* 175–239), in which Palmer and Godechot try to demonstrate the reality of an Atlantic civilization, particularly for the eighteenth century. For the many-faceted discussion of this paper, see *Atti,* pp. 565-579. Less comprehensive in scope is Franco Venturi's attempt to demonstrate the international movement of ideas in the eighteenth century. ("La circolazione delle idee," *Rassegna storica del Risorgimento,* XLI (1954), 203–222.)

For general factual background on the second half of the eighteenth century the two pertinent volumes in the Harper series are well informed and well written: L. Gershoy, *From Despotism to Revolution, 1763–1789* (New York, 1944), and C. Brinton, *A Decade of Revolution, 1789–1799* (New York, 1934). Both books are written from a European rather than a national point of view, though neither follows the more recent interpretation of the eighteenth-century revolutions. A more condensed and more recent volume is M. S. Anderson, *Europe in the Eighteenth Century, 1713–1783* (London, 1961), which is topically organized, very readable, and packed with information. M. Beloff, *The Age of Absolutism, 1660–1815* * (Harper Torchbooks, 1961) is too packed, but is interesting for an interpretation of the eighteenth century very much at variance with the "revolutionary" interpretation of Palmer and Godechot.

In the final analysis, the Palmer thesis can only be tested by examining individual revolutions or near-revolutions. A number of works bear on the situation in late eighteenth-century Great Britain. The standard comprehensive survey is J. S. Watson, *The Reign of George III, 1760–1820* (Oxford, 1960) in the *Oxford History of England.* More specifically addressed to the reform and revolutionary movements in England is S. Maccoby, *English Radicalism, 1762–1785: the Origins* (New York, 1955) and C. Robbins, *The Eighteenth-Century Commonwealthman* (Cambridge, Mass., 1959), which traces the English radical tradition from the seventeenth century onward. G. Rudé's *Wilkes and Liberty* (Oxford, 1962) focuses on the struggle for reform of the seventeen-seventies. A. Davies, "La Révolution française et le Pays de Galles," *Annales historiques de la Révolution française,* XXVII (1955), 202–212, discusses revolutionary influences in Wales. For the Irish background, a recent history is E. Curtis, *History of Ireland* (London, 1950).

Aside from Palmer's article reprinted in this volume, there is no accessible history of the Dutch revolutions. For general accounts of the period, the somewhat old-fashioned P. J. Blok, *A History of the People of the Netherlands,* V (New York, 1912), or B. H. M. Vlekke's *The Evolution of the Dutch Nation* (New York, 1945) may be consulted. For the Hapsburg domains E. Wangermann's *From Joseph II to the Jacobin Trials,* from which a selection is included in this volume, is the only full account for its period. S. K. Padover, *The Revolutionary Emperor* (New York, 1934), deals with the earlier reign of Joseph II. A number of studies have recently appeared on the revolutionary movement in eighteenth-century Hungary, such as P. F. Sugar, "The Influence of the Enlightenment and the French Revolution in Eighteenth-Century Hungary," *Journal of Central European Affairs,* XVII (1957), 331–355; Paul Bödy, "The Hungarian Jacobin Conspiracy of 1794–95," *ibid.,* XXII (1962), 3–26; R. R. Palmer and P. Kenez, "Two Documents of the Hungarian Revolutionary Movement of 1794," *ibid.,* XX (1960), 423–444; K. Benda, "Les jacobins hongrois," *Annales historiques de la Révolution française,* XXXI (1959), 38–60.

There are, of course, innumerable works on the American Revolution. J. F. Jameson, *The American Revolution Considered as a Social Movement** (Beacon, 1956) is a good starting point although, as the Tolles article included in this volume points out, some of its views must be revised. There are a number of competent recent studies on the American Revolution. B. Knollenberg, *The Origins of the American Revolution* (New York, 1960), takes a rather narrow view by concentrating on British imperial policy of the seventeen-sixties. L. H. Gipson, *The Coming of the Revolution, 1763–1755* (New York, 1954), is an up-to-date synthesis by an authority on British imperial policy. S. R. Alden, *The American Revolution, 1775–83* (New York, 1954), is another competent account in the same series. Somewhat less detailed is E. S. Morgan, *The Birth of the Republic, 1763–1789** (Chicago University Press, 1956), a volume of the "History of American Civilization." Also recommended is the even more recent *Origins of the American Revolution* (Palo Alto, 1959), by J. C. Miller. The most convenient collection of the various interpretations of the American revolutionary movement is J. C. Wahlke, ed., *The Causes of the American Revolution** (Heath, 1950).

The standard account of the French Revolution is G. Lefebvre's *La Révolution française,* the first half of which has been translated as *The French Revolution,* I, *From Its Origins to 1793* (New York, 1962), which occupies a half-way house between purely national interpretation and out-and-out "westernizing." Lefebvre recognizes and discusses the international ramifications of the revolutionary upheaval, yet he nonetheless explains the French Revolution basically in terms of French conditions. The same author's brilliant study of the advent of the revolution, entitled in English *The Coming of the French Revolution,** (Vintage, 1957), confines itself entirely to the French background. Two excellent up-to-date syntheses of the French Revolution are A. Cobban, *A History of Modern France, 1715-1799,* vol. I* (Penguin, 1957), and A. Goodwin, *The French Revolution 1789–1794** (Harper Torchbooks, 1961). Two shorter accounts which take a definite *pro* and *con* position on the Palmer thesis are J. Godechot, "The French Revolution," in *Chapters in Western Civilization* (2nd ed., New York, 1962), pp. 1–54 for the affirmative; G. Rudé, "The Outbreak of the French Revolution," *Past and Present,* No. 8, November 1955, pp. 28–42, for the negative. For the controversy surrounding the economic background of the revolution, see R. W. Greenlaw, ed., *The Economic Origins of the French Revolution—Poverty or Prosperity?* (Heath, 1958). An interesting brief survey of the gradual evolution in the interpretation of the French Revolution as influenced by the changing French political scene is P. Farmer, *France Reviews Its Revolutionary Origins* (New York, 1944).